Cover photo: Dad, my brother John, half of our dog Priney, and I at our old home in Holladay.

I'll Tell You What ...

ANN EDWARDS CANNON

Best wishes to Andrew!

Ann Edwards Cannon

Copyright © 2018 by Ann Edwards Cannon
All rights reserved, including the right to reproduce this book or portions thereof in any form whatsoever.
Printed in the United States of America
ISBN: 9781532353376

TKE Ink
www.kingsenglish.com

1511 South 1500 East
Salt Lake City UT 84105
www.kingsenglish.com

For my parents, always and again

TABLE OF CONTENTS

The Full Catastrophe — **3**
Lessons My Mother Taught Me — 5
Accommodators — 8
Stupid Girls in Stupid Bonnets
    (Notice How That Rhymes with Sonnets) — 11
The Grunions Are Coming, The Grunions Are Coming — 14
I Swear My Son Has a Good Heart — 17
Watch Out for Toxins! — 20
It's Not Like Anyone Needed That Tree Anyway — 23
Aunts Who Pole Vault — 26
Driving with Parents — 29
Life's a Beach Vacation, Baby — 32

Pets and Other Beasts — **37**
Dog Dreams — 39
Puppy Lessons — 42
Living Large with a Large Dog — 45
Hello, Tinkerbell! — 48
Sinister Sheep — 51
Jacques — 54
Snail Slayer — 57
Tiptoe Through the Tomatoes with Tinkerbell — 60

Getting My Philosophy On — **65**
Weighty Matters — 67
Losing Things — 70
Stuff I Never Have to Do Again — 73
Flossing and Other Newly Declared Evils — 76
When Things Matter — 79
I Wish You More — 82
Dear Bacon — 85
This I Believe — 88

Sports and the Whole Nine Yards — **93**
Hey Chicago, Whaddya Say! — 95
Thirty Things I Learned While Running
    the St. George Marathon Last Weekend — 98
Grandchildren at the Ballpark — 101
Meditation While Watching a Granddaughter
    (Sort of) Playing Soccer — 104
That Was Then, This Is Now — 107
How to Make Your Butt Look Big — 110

TABLE OF CONTENTS (cont.)

A Utah County Girl Am I, Sir	**115**
Dear T.S. Eliot	117
Giant Rabbit	120
Home Perms	123
Loving the Place Where You've Always Been	126
Snow Day	129
Oo La La! The French Professor and Moi!	132
Out and About	**137**
Knitting on the Beach	139
A Couple of Things I Learned While Biking Across Holland	142
Five Things I Recently Learned on a Trip to the Lone Star State	145
Thirty Things I Learned While Walking Across England	148
Dear National Park Service	152
Cows, Aliens and All That Jazz	155
Celebration Time (Come On!)	**159**
Resolutions	161
Hearts on Fire	164
What to Do on a Saturday When You're an Empty Nester in 25 Easy Steps	167
Fathers	170
And Suddenly It's the Fourth of July	173
Who Doesn't Love a Dog in Costume?	176
Thanksgiving the First	179
Fear Not	182
Throw Deep	185
I'll Tell You What	**189**
Practically a Movie Star	191
I Left My Heart There, Too	194
I'll Have a Flying Car, Please	197
Story Problems	200
Running Shoes	203
Memorial Day	206
Mental Illness	209
Green Lights	212
Hank Williams	215
Fathers and Fathers	218
How to Be Present When Someone's World Falls Apart	221
What I Miss	223
DeVan	225
Safe Passage	228
Funeral Talk	231
Peaches	236
Your People Stay With You	239

INTRODUCTION

Way back in 1985—you may remember 1985 as the year that Coca-Cola changed its original recipe and briefly foisted "New Coke" on an unwilling world—my husband, Ken Cannon, and I packed up two small children (they were ours, so don't worry) and moved to Finland for awhile where I spent a lot of time changing diapers. In other words, being in Finland was just like being in America! Only I was colder! And also I had to listen to polka music on the radio!

When we returned to the states, I wrote a column about the experience, which Patty Kimball published in Parent Express. And I've been doing a version of that column ever since, writing about family and friends and all the funny things that happen on the way to wherever you're going.

So that's what we have here. Stories I've shared with readers as a weekly columnist for The Salt Lake Tribune. I will say that this collection is particularly meaningful to me because I've included a number of memories about my father, who passed away in December of 2016.

I cannot even begin to say how much I miss him.

I'll Tell You What …

Part of the catastrophe in front of the stadium when we were all much younger.

THE FULL CATASTROPHE

Remember that movie "Zorba the Greek," based on the novel by Nikos Kazantzakis?

There's a great scene where Zorba says this: "Am I not a man? And is a man not stupid? I'm a man, so I married. Wife, children, house, everything. The full catastrophe."

I have the full catastrophe, too, although my name isn't Zorba and I'm not Greek. Also, I'm not a man.

I am, however, grateful for my full catastrophe. Most of the time.

And even when I'm not, it always provides me with material. So. Much. Material.

This section features columns inspired by family and friends, who have kindly allowed me to exploit them for lo these many years.

Thank you, Family and Friends. I love you.

The only thing missing from this photo is the puka shell necklaces my boys always wore.

LESSONS MY MOTHER TAUGHT ME

First Published March 2012

When she's in a certain mood, my mother will tell you that I never listen to her. She'll say this with exasperated affection and then shrug her shoulders because seriously now —what are you gonna do with a daughter like that?

Anyway, this amazing woman to whom I never ever listen is having herself a birthday tomorrow. A milestone birthday (although I won't tell you which milestone), so I thought I'd share with you some of the things I've learned by NOT LISTENING to my mother over the years. Here goes.

> Get a dog. Sure, you can live without one, but where's the fun in that?
> In fact, get a poodle. And then spoil him rotten.
> Take up knitting. It's great therapy.
> Advocate for children. Advocate for people who can't do it for themselves.

Root for the underdog. Unless, of course, your team is playing the underdog.
Remember that loyalty is the supreme virtue, while recognizing that loyalty can turn you stupid at times.
Make casseroles and take them in when neighbors are sick.
Never forget that while men are good with the text, you can't count on them to get the subtext.
When in need of an excuse, feel free to chalk it up to hormones.
End each meal—even breakfast—with a bite of chocolate.
Be a parent to your young children. Be a friend to your adult children.
Reside in the present moment. The past is overrated anyway.
On the other hand, you should write a personal history as a way to honor your roots.
Vote.
Love your in-laws.
Keep putting up a Christmas tree, even after the kids leave.
Don't hesitate to take on a wealthy corporation if you think that wealthy corporation is busy polluting your backyard. Or state.
Open the doors of your life and make room there for people who aren't like you.
Take care of your friends.
Keep your partner guessing.
Throw a well-timed fit now and then just to get people's attention.
Respect Wyoming and the fearsome mighty women who hail from there.
Go back to college and graduate if you feel like it. Even if

you're in your 60s and other people tell you not to bother.
Let the dishes wait.
Never be without a book or two. Or three. Or 20.
Appreciate art.
Learn how to text your grandchildren.
Remember that while clothes come and go, jewelry is forever.
Take a brisk walk every morning of your life.
Take the poodle with you, even if he protests.
Worry about your kids, no matter how old they are.
Grow houseplants, because houseplants help a person survive the winter months.
Invest in a good haircut. A good haircut won't solve your problems, but at least you can earn style points while dealing with them.
Laugh. And then laugh some more. Especially at yourself.

Well, I could go on and on. But I think I've made my point. I've been listening, even if I don't always follow my mother's advice—although I'd probably be a better person if I did.

Thanks, Mom. Happy birthday.

ACCOMMODATORS

First Published May 2017

    Today I wish to discuss something I've noticed about human beings, aka "us." But first I want to tell you about a recent road trip my mother and I took to attend her grandson's and my nephew's wedding. (Hey, congratulations, Nick and Courtney!)
    Anyway. It was just the two of us this time—sort of like Thelma and Louise, if Thelma and Louise had been members of AARP. Meanwhile, here's an example of the conversations Mom and I had along the way.
ME: Should we stop in Fillmore and get some Corn Nuts?
HER: Whatever you want to do.
ME: No. It's whatever you want to do.
HER: No. It's whatever YOU want to do.
Here's another example.
HER: Where would you like to go to dinner?
ME: I'm good with whatever. Where would you like to go to dinner?
HER: I'm good with whatever. You choose.

ME: No, seriously. YOU choose.

Or there's this one.

ME: Do you want to watch a movie or play cards tonight?

HER: Either one.

ME: Same here. Either one.

HER: Both are good choices. You choose.

ME: I agree. Both are good choices. YOU choose.

My mom and I had conversations like these on our recent road trip because both of us are "accommodators"— that is, we often feel more motivated to accommodate other people's choices than we do to accommodate our own. And if you recognize yourself in any of these conversations, you may also be an "accommodator," as well, which means by the time you and your mother decided to buy some Corn Nuts in Fillmore, you were already in Cedar City. Welcome to our club!

But that's not the point. The point is this: Typically my mom and I would say this trait is the good thing about us. We're flexible! We're sensitive to other people's needs! We're just happy to be along for the ride, and while we're along for the ride, we're not the least bit demanding! No sir, not us.

(Actually, these things are true of my mother. Me, I'm accommodating because I'm lazy. So there's that.)

Eventually, however, it occurred to me that sometimes a desire to accommodate actually complicates things rather than making them easier. There are times, for instance, when someone just needs to step up and say let's have some Thai for dinner (drunken noodles) or let's play cards tonight (even though I know you'll beat me again) or YES! BY ALL MEANS! LET'S STOP IN FILLMORE AND BUY SOME CORN NUTS (but let's get the "original" flavor, not "ranch" or "barbecue")!

Which brings me to this observation, not for the first time, about human beings. The good thing about a person can also be the difficult thing about that very same person. For example, in some contexts stubbornness can be viewed as persistence or doggedness or grit. In other contexts, however, it can just be viewed as—you know—stubbornness. Same quality. Different manifestations.

The opposite can be true, too. Take my husband, for example. He carries around a battered briefcase that roughly dates from the Mesozoic Era. At times I'll look at that briefcase and wonder why dude won't spring for a new one. But then I remember he appreciates old things—like an old wife, for example. And suddenly I find him and that briefcase pretty darn endearing.

Oh, human beings.

Still. The next time my mother and I hit the road, I think I'll hire a non-accommodator to go with us. If you're interested in the job, feel free to send resumés to me in care of this paper.

Thank you. And have a nice day.

STUPID GIRLS IN STUPID BONNETS (Notice How That Rhymes with "Sonnet")

First Published May 2011

Dear Future High School English Teachers of America,
    I am writing you this letter as a Public Service. Consider it a well-meant invitation to seriously reconsider your choice of career before it's too late.
    Why am I doing this? My youngest son, who is getting ready to graduate from West High School in a few weeks, recently unearthed a sonnet he wrote for his freshman English class. It's called "This Is About How I Hate Love Sonnets." I print it here with his permission and his blessing.
    This is about how I hate love sonnets,
    They use stupid language and metaphors:
    They have stupid girls in stupid bonnets,

Goodness, just thinking of them makes me snore.
I cannot figure out why people love them,
I can't describe why they suck, they just do:
These moronic poems are condemned,
And are simply quite splendidly untrue.
Anybody can write these stupid things,
Though some are better at it than others:
But Shakespeare's got nothing on my writings,
Though he's slightly better than my brothers'.
So long as men can breathe or eyes can see,
These poems will bring displeasure to me.

Okay. Clearly my son did not write this for fun. Clearly my son did not roll out of bed one morning and say to himself, dude! I think I'll write a sonnet today!

No. He was assigned to write one by a dedicated English teacher whose only goal was to make her students appreciate their rich literary heritage. And this is how she was rewarded. Furthermore, dear Future High School English Teachers of America, this is how you will be rewarded if you dare ask a 14-year-old male to write a love poem. Especially one that rhymes. He'll write it—if he bothers to write it at all—in a full-blown snit.

On the other hand, I have to say that I personally think this poem is kind of... awesome. Maybe it's just the mother in me or maybe it's just that I'm a natural born sucker for poems involving "stupid girls in stupid bonnets," but seriously—who can resist?

And of course I'm way interested in the fact that Shakespeare has nothing on my son. Score! In fact, I feel like getting a bumper sticker that says, "My kid writes better sonnets than Shakespeare," although in fairness I would have to get a second bumper sticker that says "Shakespeare writes better sonnets than my other kids."

But my favorite line? "I can't describe why they suck, they just do." It's hard not to admire the directness of that statement. And come on! Haven't we all felt that way about sonnets at times? Probably even you, dear Future High School English Teachers of America, have felt that way about sonnets. Especially when you were 14 years old.

Speaking of which, when my son showed me this poem, he also mentioned how much he liked the teacher who forced him to write it—Mindy Thompson. He also liked the other English teachers he's had at West High—Marcie Thompson, Julie Adams, and Fran Craigle. Why? Because they made him think, even when he didn't want to.

So okay, dear FHSETofA, never mind. Forget about this letter and carry on.

Sincerely,
Ann Cannon

THE GRUNIONS ARE COMING, THE GRUNIONS ARE COMING

First Published July 2014

My family—parents, siblings, spouses, everybody's kids—have been going to the same beach together for nearly 30 years now, and it was on one of those first trips that my youngest brother told us about grunions.

Because I am tragically lacking in the Essential Fish 411 department, he brought me up to speed. Grunions, he explained, are tiny fish that mate on the sandy shores of southern California. If you walk along the beach at night when they're running, you can find thousands of grunions making out like teenagers in the moonlight—sighing and moaning and accidentally bumping their noses together when attempting an awkward kiss.

This all sounded frankly suspicious to me. Really? I asked my brother. Are you sure "grunion" isn't just another word for "snipe?"

You remember snipe hunts, don't you? Somebody hands you a bag at a slumber party and tells you to go find some snipes in the neighbor's bushes, which you do until the neighbor shows up on his front porch wearing grumpy-old-man pajama bottoms and yells at you to get off his lawn. Which of course you do because neighbors in grumpy-old-man pajama bottoms are reliably scary. Meanwhile everyone else is next door having a good laugh at your expense. Hahahahaha!

So yeah. That's what I figured grunions were. Snipes.

Still, year after year I went out on the beach at midnight with my brother and his kids, looking for the elusive grunions.

And then one night, there they were, sliding out of the ocean's foam and onto the slick sand. Grunions! Grunions! Grunions! Miles and miles of them, storming the seashore like tiny marines mounting an invasion of epic proportions. First they would secure their location on the beach. And then they would take over the city, after which they would move onto the capital in Sacramento and assume control over the entire state of California. ATTENTION, HUMANS OF CALIFORNIA! THE GRUNIONS ARE IN CHARGE NOW! IT IS FUTILE TO RESIST.

My nephews—all of them little boys still—went crazy at the sight of all those tiny fish. They charged into the waves like David Hasselhoff and grabbed handfuls of them—laughing as the fish slipped through their fingers and back into the salty water, stuffing the rest into the pockets of their shorts.

I even barehanded a few myself and felt them flip against the hollow of my hand before I released them. It was an awesome feeling, actually—like I was some big old crazypants

Grizzly Bear spearing myself some salmon. Except that my salmon were only two inches long. But whatever.

Anyway. It was a memorable evening. And I could officially remove "grunions" from the List of Things I Don't Believe in Anymore. Grunions are real, people. They exist.

I haven't seen the grunions run since that evening, although I always visit the beach after dark in hopes I'll see them again. I walked along the familiar shore again just last week hoping for a glimpse of them, glistening silver with the moon on their backs.

I didn't see them. Sometimes I doubt I ever will again.

But what I did see were the ghosts of who we used to be. My brother. Me. And especially his sons who are now turning into men. I could see those boys leap into the mighty yawn of the Pacific Ocean and hear them shriek with remembered laughter as night water splashed up to greet them.

Their hands squirming with strange lovely treasure.

I SWEAR MY SON HAS A GOOD HEART

First Published July 2013

    Oh, it's just AMAZING what you'll find when you finally get around to cleaning underneath your kids' beds after they've moved out. The sports section from the newspaper. An old rawhide chew toy. A popsicle stick. The cat. A stray Christmas ornament or two. Unmatched socks. A ninja turtle action figure. Another cat who wants to start a fight with the first cat. A pair of boxers. That report on raptors that never got turned in. Your son's old "Swear Box."
    Wait. What?
    Yes. You read that right. Swear Box. I knew it was a "Swear Box" rather than just an ordinary Nike shoebox because it had the words "Swear Box" scrawled in black marker across the top. There was also a list of swear words with a dollar amount written out for each one on the lid. In addition, there was a hole where the offender (aka "my son") could drop some money any time he swore.

Okay. Let me make some observations about this surprising discovery.

The first observation is that I was actually proud of my son for taking on a project like this with zero parental involvement. Trust me. I had no idea he was doing this, nor would I have encouraged him to proceed, because then I would have felt obligated to stop swearing myself.

So yeah. He gets full points from me for making a completely independent move on the self-improvement front.

The second observation is that I was actually impressed by his range of expression. Who knew there were so many words? Isn't English an awesome language that way? And so flexible, too! You gotta love a language where a word can be any part of speech you need it to be.

What really intrigued me were the dollar amounts ascribed to each word, ranging from 25 cents to $5.00. I was relieved to see that my favorite go-to swear word only costs 25 cents to use. It's a humble, garden-variety swear word that is nonetheless useful in a variety of situations, not unlike the miniature Swiss Army pocket knife you always carry in your purse, except, of course, when you're going through Security at the airport. Unless, of course, you forget to take it out of your purse. Again.

I was surprised, however, by one of the $2.00 words—a word I have been known to say without (apparently) realizing it's a $2.00 word, which leads me to wonder if I've turned into the mom in our neighborhood where I grew up who used the word "bitchin" because she was from Switzerland and didn't know what the word meant. So if I have used that $2.00 word in front of you, please forgive me. Although if you're my age, chances are good you didn't know it was a $2.00 word either.

Anyway. As you can imagine I was eager to see if there was any money in the box. And there wasn't. There was, however, a boatload of IOU's—some for as much as $15.00, because you know how it is. Some days are just $15.00 days.

Which caused me to call up my son and ask these questions.

ME: Did you ever plan to replace those IOU's with actual money?
SON: Yes. At first.
ME: What were you going to do with the actual money?
SON: Give it to the Salvation Army.

Obviously he never followed up with that part of the plan, but still. I swear (ha!) you gotta love a kid whose heart is in the right place.

WATCH OUT FOR TOXINS!

First Published June 2016

DATELINE: SOUTHERN CALIFORNIA

Yesterday we took two of our grandkids to Disneyland. When we boarded the Pirates of the Caribbean boat, our 6-year-old granddaughter took it upon herself to warn fellow passengers about the hazards that awaited them. "YOU MIGHT GET WET!" she said. "ALSO, IF YOU'RE AFRAID OF PIRATES, CLOSE YOUR EYES!"

But my favorite thing she said was this: "WATCH OUT FOR TOXINS!"

Toxins?

Where did that come from?

The more I thought about it, however, the more sense her warning made to me. Seriously, this world is filled with all kinds of toxins. Physical toxins. Emotional toxins. Intellectual toxins. And being able to recognize them and the forms they take is an excellent life skill. So when I sat down to write my column first thing this morning, I decided to list all the things I hope my granddaughter will avoid as she makes her way into adulthood, such as prolonged exposure to the Kardashians.

But then I heard the pounding of waves against the sand. I inhaled thick air scented with salt and saw the sky spread like a smile over the Pacific Ocean, and I wrote this letter instead.

Dear Bean,

You are now old enough and smart enough to understand that life can be scary. That's why you were warning us on the boat. People who recall childhood as a purely carefree, magical time aren't remembering its very real terrors—the nightmares, the casual and not-so-casual bullying, the complete dependence on people older and bigger than you, the lack of control over your own emotions.

As you grow older, you'll discover more things to fear. Some of those fears will grow out of internal anxiety rather than any real threat to you or the people you love. But some of those fears will be legitimate.

That's why I want you to remember this: no matter what happens, the world is a profoundly beautiful place. Carry this knowledge with you always and learn to draw upon it when you feel afraid. Keep your senses engaged and rediscover the natural world around you every day.

> See the colors and shapes of plants. In particular, notice the varying shades of green—silver and moss and olive and kelly.
>
> Step out onto your porch at night and track the phases of the moon.
>
> Hear the conversations of birds and watch the patterns of flight they weave.
>
> Feel cool grass beneath your bare feet and warm sun in your hair.
>
> Run your hand over a lavender plant on a morning walk

and carry the scent home with you.

Learn to smell a rainstorm before the rain even falls.

And while you're noticing the natural world, watch the people who inhabit it, especially when they perform small thoughtful acts for one another—holding the door open for a stranger, taking a meal in to someone who's ill, distracting a fussy baby to give the mother a break, giving directions to someone who's lost, laughing at a kid's knock-knock joke even if it isn't funny, holding someone's hand, paying for the guy behind you in the line at McDonald's, mowing a neighbor's lawn week after week (thanks, Joe).

These are small things, yes. But in my experience, taking the time to notice them can act as a partial antidote to hopelessness and to fear.

Meanwhile, Bean, carry on. I'm so glad I get to be a part of your journey. And thanks for warning me about the pirates.

Fondly,

Tutu

IT'S NOT LIKE ANYONE NEEDED THAT TREE ANYWAY

First Published March 2015

    The problem with making a friend when you're 11 years old is that you have no idea who that friend will be when she grows up. With any luck that friend will turn into a teacher or a medical professional or a travel agent or a personal shopper or a stay-at-home mom or a businesswoman or a bookseller—someone with whom all your girlhood secrets are safe.
    OR!
    She could grow up to be a writer.
    Here's the deal. If you have anybody in your life who shows any inclination to write, you should turn around and run—now. Pack your bags. Head for the hills. Get out of Dodge. Abandon ship. Slip out the back, Jack. Make a new plan, Stan. Skedaddle! Flee! BEFORE IT'S TOO LATE!

Why, you ask?

Because writers write about what they know, including the people they know. *Especially* the people they know.

They write about their fathers and how those fathers took one look at math assignments, handed them back, and said that children should do their own story problems, thank you very much.

They write about their mothers and how they were a (scary) force to be reckoned with whenever they got their Wyoming cowgirl on.

They write about their brothers and how they used to dress those brothers up like girls and make them fetch the mail so the neighbors would think those brothers were actually sisters.

They write about their dogs and how those dogs knocked over Christmas trees in the backroom when they thought no one was looking.

They write about their mothers' dogs and how their mothers' dogs stole pork chops right off of dinner plates when they thought no one was looking.

They write about sons and how those sons all went commando to the pediatrician's office that one day.

They write about husbands and how those husbands cheer—year after futile year—for the reliably awful Chicago Cubs. (Cue his favorite joke—"Everyone can have an off-century!")

And yes. Writers write about friends that they made when they were both 11 years old.

Writers will write about how super nerdy the two of you were in the sixth grade, reading *A Wrinkle in Time* like it was the *Holy Bible* and playing "The Green Berets" on your ukuleles. (?!!) Or how embarrassed you were that your mothers showed up to register you for your classes like you were babies on the first day of seventh grade. Or how you both ran for class office in junior high school and lost, which caused the two of you to cry and cry and cry. Or how you got mixed up and accidentally washed your hair with Avon's Skin-So-Soft bath oil instead of shampoo.

Writers will write about that day the two of you got busted eating tacos (with a side of frijoles) at Taco Bell by the writer's dad when you were both supposed to be somewhere else. Or how you used to watch Milo White snarf Jell-O in the school cafeteria. Or (most famously) how you single-handedly took down a tree at the Provo High School driver's ed range, which caused your driver's ed teacher, Mr. Moon, to regard you forever after with both respect and fear.

Writers, in other words, will write about YOU.

Are you up for that?

If you are, then my hope is that you will be as good a sport about it as my fabulous friend Gigi Ballif Arrington has been for lo these many years.

Happy birthday, Gigi.

I couldn't love you more—but please let me drive. (I insist.)

AUNTS WHO POLE VAULT

First Published February 2012

So I've written before about my grandmother's sisters Bea and Blanche, who were about as different from one another as two women could be. Bea was Tigger. Blanche was Eeyore.

In spite of their differences, however, they seemed to get along with one another well enough—except for that one time I took them (along with my grandmother) to the mall to buy some fish and chips. We discovered we were missing an order after sitting down, so then Bea asked Blanche where the Happy Halibut went and Blanche said she didn't know and who did we think she was anyway—the Happy Halibut police?

Words were exchanged. And after Bea realized Blanche was actually sitting on the missing order, MORE words were exchanged.

But whatever. That's not the point. I'm sure aunts accidentally sit on orders of fish and chips all the time. The real point is this: I recently went to a viewing with my parents where we ran into an elderly couple who knew Blanche's family. When the husband figured out that Blanche and I were related, he said almost the last thing I would have ever expected someone to say about my great aunt.

"Did you know Blanche was a champion pole-vaulter?" he asked me.

I was dumbstruck.

Wait. What? My Aunt Blanche was a champion pole-vaulter? I immediately texted this surprising information to my brother who lives in Las Vegas.

JIMMY: Wow. I didn't even know pole-vaulting was invented back then.

ME: The only thing that would have surprised me more is to learn she'd been a champion pole dancer.

JIMMY: This could create a whole new line of family jokes. Why did Aunt Blanche choose the pole vault for her event?

ME: Why?

JIMMY: Because the 100-yard dash in a prairie skirt was too hard.

I know. Hahahahahaha. And just for the record, I fully expect our great-nephews and nieces will be making up jokes about me and my brother one day, too.

Still. I've been thinking a lot about my pole-vaulting aunt, sailing over a high bar while shouting YOLO beneath a blue bright sky. I wish I'd known about her life as an athlete. The information might have made me see her a little differently when she was still alive.

This experience has also led me to consider (once again) how many of our family stories we never hear. Seriously, if you'd been a champion pole-vaulter in your youth, wouldn't you want all your kinfolk to know? So why not generate a list called "Things About Me That Might Surprise You" and encourage the people in your family to do the same.

My list would look something like this:
1. I won a purple ribbon at the State Fair for some random eggplants I grew in my backyard one summer.
2. I was in the fourth grade when my dad realized I didn't know the difference between my left hand and my right hand.
3. I love to read, but I am actually a slow reader.
4. I almost majored in dance when I was a freshman in college, because I wanted to be just like my teacher Abby Fiat.
5. I do crossword puzzles in ink—not because I'm good at them but because I'm too lazy to sharpen a pencil.
6. I once wrote a Harlequin romance under the pen name "Lucinda Lawson." It was rejected.
7. I got a D in Driver's Ed. But at least I didn't take out a tree like my friend Gigi Ballif did that time she put the car in "forward" instead of "reverse."
8. I was a champion pole-vaulter.
9. Kidding!
10. That was my Aunt Blanche.

MORAL OF THIS STORY: Share your own stories. Write them down. Do it!

DRIVING WITH PARENTS

First Published August 2016

Dear My Adult Kids,
    I want you to listen up. Why, you ask? Because I am going to share an important universal truth with you today.
    But first I want to tell you about this weekend and how I drove your grandparents (my parents) to Las Vegas from St. George.
    DO NOT SKIP OVER THIS PART BECAUSE IT'S IMPORTANT.
    And also you should always listen to what I say because all of it is important. But whatever.
    Anyway. The three of us decided to go to Vegas to see your Uncle Jimmy and his family, but when your grandparents (my parents) got tired, I offered to take over the driving part.
    Now here's the thing: when I slid behind the steering wheel, I sensed a certain unease on their part, which I found confusing. Why should my parents be uneasy? It's not like I've never driven distances before.

For example, with the help of sons, I have made several cross-country road trips, and I have driven solo plenty of times, too, including that one trip to Oregon when (okay, fine) my car's water tank blew up and I rode into Eugene with a tow truck guy who told me how he delivered his girlfriend's baby by himself which made me very happy that he and his tow truck weren't anywhere nearby when I delivered one of my own babies.

But that's not the point.

The point is I could tell that my father (sitting in the front passenger seat) and my mother (sitting in the backseat with a poodle) were nervous. Especially my mother. She kept reminding me to observe the speed limits even though she has a lead foot herself. Also, whenever I changed lanes, I could hear a sharp intake of breath from somewhere in the backseat, and I'm assuming it wasn't the poodle stressing.

My father, on the other hand, looked like a man who has seen way, way, way too much of life. His expression was one of epic stoicism as he clutched the hand rest and looked grimly out of the windshield.

This made me want to say, "What is up with you two? I haven't gotten a ticket for years! Especially if you don't count that time I got pulled over by the UHP and I couldn't find my registration in the glove compartment although I did find an expired coupon for some Lunchables. So what's your problem?"

And then I realized what was happening.

When I was a teenager living with your grandparents (my parents) I collected tickets the way some people collect those little teaspoons from different states. I also ran into other cars, sometimes while wearing a drill uniform, although it is true I wasn't wearing one of those when I ran into our neighbor Tom Brown's VW bug. I was just wearing regular clothes then.

Also, there was that time I made a sudden, unexpected stop with my father sitting in the front seat, which caused him to go crashing into the dashboard as a thousand empty Tab bottles went soaring past his ears because we were on our way to Carson's Market to return them for a deposit.

So there the three of us were this weekend. My mother and a poodle in the backseat. My father in the front seat with a face looking like it had been carved into Mount Rushmore. Me behind the steering wheel.

And it occurred to me then that at some level, they possibly still think of me as that idiot kid who had terrible car karma.

Who can blame them?

So what's the universal truth I referred to earlier? You guys are all grown up now. But, trust me, there will be moments when I'll treat YOU like you're still the kids I remember.

As Simba (or whoever) once said. It's the circle of life.

Sincerely,
Mom

LIFE'S A BEACH VACATION, BABY

First Published July 2016

My brothers, our families, our parents and I have now been going to the beach together every summer for a million years. This has made me something of an expert when it comes to the trajectory family vacations tend to follow. Take a look and see if any of this sounds familiar to you.

SATURDAY: Yay! You've all arrived at the beach! THE BEACH! THE BEACH! THE BEACH! Stow your stuff in the beach house (including all that toilet paper you bought at Costco before you left Utah because there might not be any toilet paper in California) and hit the sand ASAP for the remaining hours of daylight. THE BEACH! THE BEACH! THE BEACH!

SUNDAY: Wake up with the sun. Go buy some donuts. Also some cronuts. THANK YOU, SOMEBODY, FOR

INVENTING CRONUTS. Cronuts are genius! Take a bike ride. Take a walk. Take another bike ride. Take another walk. Get in the water. Get out of the water. Get in the water. Get out of the water. Life is good. Good! Good! Good! And you are more than just a little giddy because you are at THE BEACH!

MONDAY: Ah yeah. Another day in Paradise. Dude. Why do you even live in Utah when you could live in Paradise? Celebrate another day in Paradise by staying outside all day long and getting burned.

TUESDAY: Still pretty much Paradise. But okay. That burn stings. So stay inside for part of the day and play cards. Tell the same story you've told for years about how your son and your niece used to cheat at cards when they were in grade school. It was always a big old Cheat-Off when those two got together. Also remind people to deal to their left so they won't get shot in Vegas. Meanwhile, make plans to go to Disneyland the next day. YAY FOR DISNEYLAND! YAY FOR DISNEYLAND CORNDOGS! THANK YOU, SOMEBODY, FOR INVENTING DISNEYLAND CORNDOGS! Disneyland corndogs are genius! Meanwhile, Wednesday seems like the perfect day to go to Disneyland because it's in the middle of the week. It'll be less crowded! You guys are genius!

WEDNESDAY: YAY, DISNEYLAND! But wait. Even though it's Wednesday, it's still crowded. Also hot. Also expensive. But still! It's Disneyland! SO YAY! Put on some mouse ears and go buy yourself a corndog!

THURSDAY: OK. If somebody's gonna have a meltdown on

this trip, it'll happen today. By Thursday there's been just a little too much of everything, including sand in the bottom of your swimming suit. Gah! Why does most of the beach end up in the bottom of your swimming suit every year?

Nerves can be frayed by Thursday. Blowups occur. Meanwhile, everybody remembers YOUR epic meltdown a few years ago when you forgot you were a grownup and you made your mother pull over so you could jump out of the car because you were in a snit, which made your sister-in-law and nieces sitting in the back seat go hey! What the hell just happened here?

Yup. It's Thursday.

FRIDAY: Wait! What?! It's Friday already? Beach Week is almost over? Didn't you just unload all that toilet paper from Costco out of the car? How can Beach Week be almost over? This reality is greeted with a potent mixture of melancholy . . . and relief. Meanwhile, everybody starts reminiscing about the past week like it's already in the distant past. Then you eat some farewell donuts. Also cronuts.

SATURDAY AGAIN: Time to leave. Hugs all around. Maybe even a few tears. Meanwhile, everybody agrees. BEST BEACH WEEK EVER, PEOPLE!

See you next year!

Ken Cannon with his mother, Ruth, and sisters Connie, Ruth Lynne, Nancy, and Jeri.

RIP, Zora

PETS AND OTHER BEASTS

My dad used to joke that where my mother was concerned, he came in third place. The kids came in first. The dogs came in second. My dad, meanwhile, took home the Bronze.

There was never any question, in my mind at least, that Dad came first in Mom's heart. Still. We always had dogs at our house. And cats. And birds and guinea pigs and hamsters and lizards, too. Mom was crazy about all of them.

Just like I was, too. And still am.

In this section, you'll find columns about encounters with animals, both domestic and wild. Sometimes it's hard to tell them apart.

One of our babies being kissed by a cocker. My mom always hated this picture because—germs!

My brother John and I in pajamas with pets.

DOG DREAMS

First Published November 2015

    The other night I dreamed I opened the front door and my old childhood dog Brutus streaked outside and down the street like a greased pig at the Iowa State Fair.

    Brutus was a Boston Terrier with a slick black-and-white coat and neat prick ears, which made him look like he was wearing a top hat and tails—sort of like Fred Astaire, yo. That's where the resemblance ended, however, because UNLIKE Fred Astaire (yo), half of Brutus's body was head, which meant that he fell forward a lot and did somersaults whenever he started running. But then he'd spring back up on those spindly, popsicle-stick legs and commence with the running thing all over again.

    Speaking of which—one Sunday afternoon when we were out walking, my mom and I watched Brutus, who was racing ahead of us, get run over by a pickup.

    Don't judge. Nobody put their dogs on leashes back in the Dark Ages when I grew up.

    Anyway. My Mom and I screamed and clutched each

other, as screaming people often do. But then we realized that the truck had only passed over him. So after rolling around like a tumbleweed a few times, Brutus popped back up in the middle of the street and trotted toward us, totally unfazed.

Seriously. That dog was like Rasputin. You could have sicced the entire Imperial Russian court on him with knives and sabers and poison and balalaikas and he would have straight up refused to die. Yes! Now that I think about it, that's exactly what Brutus was like. A Russian monk. Yes! Brutus was a Russian monk dog.

But here's the deal. My brothers and I were nuts about Brutus, mainly because you could always count on him to bring the crazy.

Back to my dream. Like I said, I dreamed that Brutus ran out the door and down the street. So I went looking for him in the all the little alleys and side streets of Salt Lake City until (finally!) I came to a church house. I went inside and found church ladies wearing aprons in the kitchen, making funeral potatoes. I asked if they'd seen my dog and they said yes. He was in the closet.

I was overjoyed. I went to the closet and found a Boston Terrier there. I picked him up and realized right away it wasn't Brutus. This other dog's head was too small, and besides he had bat ears like one of Martha Stewart's fancy French bulldogs. I took him home anyway.

I know why I had this dream. Last week we had to put down our big brown Newfoundland, Zora. All the boys (except for the one who lives in Texas) came home to say goodbye. There were tears, of course, although I didn't cry much. I've done this enough to know that for me the tears and the missing part—those moments when you expect an animal you love to be lying on her back in the kitchen like

she always did—come later.
RIP, Zora. I'm grateful you were ours.

PUPPY LESSONS

First Published September 2014

    My husband and I are currently the foster parents (another story for another day) of a 5-month-old field spaniel, which means I've been thumbing through books about dogs recently, including a new one called *Really Important Stuff My Dog Has Taught Me* by Cynthia Copeland.
    Lessons the author has learned include the following:
*Be patient with the ones you love
*Stay close to the people who matter the most
*Leap higher than you have to
*Don't feel obligated to act your age
*Every meal is the best meal ever
*Shake it off
*Never pretend to understand if you really don't
*Keep digging until you find what you're looking for
*Greet loved ones with enthusiasm whether they've been gone 10 minutes or 10 months
    It's a good-natured little book, full of charming photos of happy dogs, and it has inspired me to write a book

specifically about puppies, who (as it turns out) spend a LOT of time trying to get your attention, which is why I'll call my book *How to Get Someone's Attention: Life Lessons I Learned from Our New Puppy.* Here are a few suggestions:

1. Wait until someone tells you NOT to leap onto the bed. Then leap onto the bed.
2. Dash into the nearest open closet and re-emerge with a shoe. In your mouth.
3. Tackle people's shoelaces as they attempt to walk from room to room. Expect to be praised for your efforts.
4. Get into a fight with the mop when somebody is mopping the kitchen floor. Dude. That mop needs to know who's boss.
5. Locate the morning paper before anybody else does. And shred it to bits.
6. Devour a book. Literally!
7. Chew up a computer cord. Because chewing up an actual chew toy is such a cliche.
8. Actually, why not just chew up everything in sight?
9. Eat all the cat's food. Then chase the cat.
10. Eat all the other cat's food. Then chase the other cat.
11. Aren't you glad you live at a house where there are two cats?
12. Also, there's an older dog who lives in the house, too. Climb on top of her head and bite her ears.
13. Howl like your heart is broken whenever someone puts you in a crate. Every. Single. Time.
14. Find a roll of toilet paper. Then festoon the house with it. Party on, people!
15. Jump up on people when they walk through the front door. Give yourself extra points for getting tangled up in their legs and tripping them.
16. Tip over wastebaskets. Because tipping over

wastebaskets is awesome!

17. Bark at the air. Someone has to.

18. Unravel an afghan that someone's been crocheting, because seriously. Does the world really need more granny squares?

    Listen, if a puppy can get all kinds of attention for engaging in these behaviors, think about how much more attention you'll get as a human being if you do exactly the same thing! Yessir, I can totally promise that people will be talking about you all day long.

    You're welcome!

    So yes. Puppies are a big plateful of Crazy with a generous helping of Fruitcake on the side. And before you invite one into your life, you need to know that. Or at least remember it.

    Still, I wouldn't mind doing this puppy thing again. And again. Then I'd do it all over again.

    And yes. I know. That officially makes me a nutball, too.

LIVING LARGE WITH A LARGE DOG

First Published July 2013

    I went to a professional conference last week where I wanted to appear—you know—professional. So I went around wearing my professional nametag, giving people professional handshakes while making professional-type observations such as "I sure hope they feed us during the breaks."

    Anyway, I totally nailed the professional thing... until I went into the bathroom and noticed I had dried dog slobber on my jacket. A lot of it. Well, hello there, folks! Nothing says "professional" like "dried dog slobber on your jacket!"

    You couldn't miss it, and I'm sure people didn't. Except for me. Apparently I forgot to check myself in the mirror one last time after our Newfoundland, Zora, gave me a goodbye kiss earlier that morning.

    Okay, in case you too have wandered around in public with large animal slobber on your clothing (and who hasn't?)

you may be interested in the following "Tips for Living With a Dog so Huge and So Hairy that People Think Bigfoot Resides at your House."

You're welcome!

1. ALWAYS check yourself in the mirror one last time after your dog gives you a goodbye kiss. (See above.)
2. Wipe your dog's mouth often. Preferably with a beach towel.
3. Invest in an industrial-strength vacuum cleaner because there will be dog hair, people. Oh yes. There will be hair.
4. Also invest in an industrial-strength washing machine. You know. Like the kind they use in institutions such as hospitals or prisons. You're gonna need that, too.

I'm not kidding. You'll find drool everywhere. On the floor. On the walls. Even on the ceilings, so yeah. Have fun with that!

Drool isn't the only issue you'll encounter when living with a giant dog, however. For one thing, giant dogs take up a lot of room. When Zora stretches out on the floor, she pretty much reaches from here to Mainland China. Furthermore, she doesn't always get up and move when you tell her to. It's not that she's willfully disobedient. Zora's just really, really busy . . . lying there. "Just lying there," in fact, features prominently on her daily To-Do list.

In light of these things, plenty of people wonder why we bother with a big dog. One thing's certain—it's not for protection. If someone broke into our house, Zora would lift her head, look at the intruder, and go, "Seriously, dude? You don't have anything better to do with your time?" Then she'd drop her head and go straight back to sleep.

So it's hard to explain why we own such a big dog. Still. I can't imagine our lives without her. There's something comforting about her presence. It's solid. Really solid. And

huge. Really huge.
 I love her chill attitude, too, which is like, "Hey. Don't sweat the small stuff. And it's all small stuff. Except for me. Just lying here. In the middle of your kitchen. Hoping to ingest some stray potato chips in much the same way a whale ingests plankton."
 Also! Her eyes! When Zora leans into me and looks up, my heart melts, not unlike cheese fondue in that avocado-green fondue pot my mom had back in the 1970s. "I'm all yours," her expression says, and you know what?
 She's right.

HELLO, TINKERBELL!

First Published March 2016

When a cherished pet dies, there are two ways to respond.

You can decide not to invite another pet into your life because the thought of losing it—and loss is ALWAYS part of the package deal when it comes to animals—is too unsettling.

Or you can, in spite of it all, acquire another cat or dog or bird or whatever it was that caught up your heart in the first place.

As far as I'm concerned, both of these responses are acceptable. No one gets to tell you how to feel or what to do. It's your call.

Having said that, I've always fallen squarely into the second camp—which is the reason why there's been such a long line of animals who've taken up residence (on the couch, usually) at chez Cannon. I'm like my mother that way. She never said no to anything we brought home. Dogs. Cats. Hamsters. Guinea Pigs. Rabbits. Birds. Lizards. Turtles. Fish. She didn't even object when I gave my youngest brother a rat for Christmas one year because you know how it is! Nothing says Merry Christmas like a pet rat!

Anyway. The point is that when one of our pets has died, I've always been willing to welcome another one into our home—that is until our big brown Newfoundland dog, Zora, died last fall.

When people asked afterwards if we were going to get another Newf, I said no. Owning a dog that weighs more than you do is not a casual commitment. Also, Newfs are not tidy animals, mostly because THEY'RE DOGS. Unlike cats, dogs don't sit around grooming themselves all day. In fact, when it comes to personal hygiene, dogs are totally the 10-year-old boys of the animal kingdom.

Newfies are especially messy. They drip water after drinking. They shed. They track mud across your kitchen floor with their Sasquatch-sized paws. They drool. Also, they drool. Then they drool some more. And after they drool, they shake it off. They just shake, shake, shake it off.

But here's the real reason I told people I didn't want another Newf. Zora was a singular animal, a unique and enormous (!) presence in our home. She presided over the living room like the Sphinx of Giza, regarding all who entered with amber leonine eyes. And when we walked down the street, traffic stopped. You could see people's mouths move. "That dog looks like a bear!"

How do you replace an animal like that?

The answer is, you don't.

But then one day I noticed how much I missed a big dog leaning into me as I folded clothes or sorted through the mail or stood at the kitchen sink. Yup. I missed the Big Dog Lean.

It's true you can never replace something you've loved. In fact, you shouldn't try. But why deny yourself the pleasure of another companion, one who's both familiar and fresh?

You can see where this is going, right?

We have a new Newfie at our house. A black female puppy. We sit around and listen to her grow. She'll be big one day. Huge! Which is why we named her Tinkerbell.

Who doesn't love a fairy that makes the walls shake whenever she tumbles into a room?

SINISTER SHEEP

First Published July 2012

    In last week's column I mentioned that sheep can sometimes come across as surprisingly sinister, and I ended up taking a little heat for that comment. Sheep? REALLY?! So now I feel compelled to explain myself.

    On the fourth day of the Great Walk Across England, my friends and I found ourselves completely alone on a windy isolated moor dotted by a thousand sheep. Everywhere you looked, you could see sheep. Sheep here. Sheep there. Vats of sheep. Layer cakes of sheep. Big old gift baskets of sheep. Sheep, sheep, sheep.

    To paraphrase that old Steely Dan song, there were sheep to the left of us, sheep to the right. There we were—stuck in the middle of sheep.

    Of course we were well acquainted with sheep by then. Northern England is a highly sheep-intensive region of the planet, and we'd already spent three days slogging through muddy pastures where the sheep behaved exactly the way you'd expect sheep to behave. Even though we came in peace and wanted to "friend" them on Facebook, as soon as we'd approach, the sheep would get all nervous and go DON'T EAT US! DON'T EAT US! Then they'd scamper out of our way, bumping into each other like they were The Three Stooges.

And we'd stand there, watching them while shaking our heads, because seriously—sheep are just so stupid.

But those sheep on the windy, isolated moor? Those sheep were a breed apart. Those sheep were NOT afraid of us. Not one little bit. They didn't run for cover when we approached. Instead, they just stood there, insolently blocking our path, regarding us with bright yellow eyeballs.

Did you catch that part?

Bright. Yellow. Eyeballs.

Bright. Yellow. Stephen King creature-type. Eyeballs.

One sheep in particular was super intimidating. It's almost like he was saying, "Yeah, everybody thinks sheep are so meek and so mild, like we're not capable of going rogue. Well, guess what. EVERYBODY IS WRONG, because me and my homeboys here? We're bad to the bone."

By this time, the wooden markers telling us which direction to head were few and far between. In fact, I was truly worried that we'd taken a wrong turn somewhere and that we were going to be lost for good—just like the Roman Ninth Legion, in which case Hollywood would one day make a movie about us starring that kid who played Billy Elliot, as well as Channing Tatum, who (it must be said) looks way better in a toga than I do. So at least there was that to be happy about.

I was also worried that the alpha sheep mocking me with his scary yellow eyeballs could smell my fear with his scary sheep nostrils, because animals can do that—smell the fear dripping off of you like cheap cologne. It's almost as though he was saying, "Take a look around you, Sister. There are no other humans in these parts for miles and miles. We could totally take you right here, right now. No one would ever know. And no one would ever suspect . . . THE SHEEP."

(AUTHOR'S NOTE: The sheep was saying this in a British accent, btw, which was awesome.)

Anyway. After accepting a substantial bribe, the sheep finally let us pass, although he continued to hoot his derision at us, as well as insult our mothers. I made it to the end of Hadrian's Wall, however, and lived to tell. Which I just did.

And now that I have, I will never speak of the Sinister Sheep Episode ever again.

JACQUES

First Published January 2011

    If I were to describe my relationship on Facebook with my mother's poodle (because isn't that what you do on Facebook? Describe your relationship with your mother's poodle?), I'd say "it's complicated."
    Before last week, however, I would have said, "Hello! It's not complicated at all. I HATE my mother's poodle, because that dog has completely supplanted me in her affections."
    You know how poodles are. Sneaky. They are just the sneaky sneak sneak-meisters of the dog world. Here's the typical Poodle M.O. He'll stand on the front porch with your parents as they wave good-bye to you.
    "Have fun in college!" your parents will say fondly. "We'll miss you, and we'll never forget you! Especially now that we're paying all that tuition!"
    Meanwhile, the poodle will look stricken. He'll even whimper a little. "Oh, I am tres triste that you are leaving us, mon amie," he'll say in Poodle Talk. "We have had such good times as a petite famille, non?"

Perhaps you'll be taken in by the melting look in his eyes. But make no mistake. The second you drive out of sight— The. Poodle. Will. Make. His. Move.

From that moment on, it's just a big old power grab. The poodle will mount a full frontal assault on your parents' affections until he has completely captured their hearts and kicked everyone else out. Including you! Their only daughter!

What gives the poodle his awesome power? Answer: he knows deep in his poodle bones that my friend Jeanne was right when she made the following observation in a recent e-mail: "children may come and go, but dogs are forever."

I knew my mother's poodle was top dog when the three of us—my mother, my mother's poodle and I—took a trip to Bear Lake together a few summers ago. I became carsick as we made our way up Logan Canyon, so I rolled down the window to get a little fresh air. As soon as I did, however, the poodle coughed. He sounded so much like Derek Zoolander, that I almost expected him to say, "I got the black lung, Ma." Only in French, of course.

My mother turned to me and said (not in French), "Yeah, I think we should roll up that window now."

Is it any surprise that I'm bitter? I ask you!

Well, through a combination of circumstances, I found myself babysitting my mother's poodle in a St. George condo last week. (Which, why am I not living in St. George? It was sunny and almost warm.) (And also, yes, it's true. I am a good daughter.)

Anyhoo! Sometime during our first night there, the poodle and his Pauley D haircut crawled into bed with me. When I awoke, I found him resting his head on the pillow next to mine.

When he heard me stir, the poodle turned and looked

straight into my eyes. Meltingly.

"Well, well, well," he said in Poodle Talk, "life is just full of little surprises, n'est-ce pas?"

Okay. I REALLY hate to say this, but guess what. I ... kinda like that dog now, because you know how life is.

(Just like the poodle said.)

SNAIL SLAYER

First Published August 2015

    Attention all snails!
    This is ME giving YOU fair warning. You have a new predator on the horizon and it's not (as Dave Barry once joked) the French.
    Are you afraid yet? Because you should be. In fact, you should be very, very afraid. Your new predator is relentless when she puts her mind to something. Do you hear me? RELENTLESS.
    How do I know this?
    Because she's my mother.
    Over the years I have watched this woman complete impossible jigsaw puzzles that everybody else abandoned long ago. I have watched her play cards late into the night with her grandchildren until everybody fell asleep at the table. Except for her. I have seen her knit sweaters from patterns so complicated that they (the patterns) make Professional Sweater Knitters weep.
    You hear what I'm saying? This is a woman who does not

give up.

And now my mother, aka "the Snail Huntress," has decided to come after you and your kin, and she'll keep coming after you and your kin until she has obliterated you from the face of the earth. Why? Because you crossed a boundary, my slimy little friends. You've recently invaded her garden. You killed her marigolds. PREPARE TO DIE!

See, here's the deal. My mother lives in Provo where I swear that your kind didn't exist while I was growing up there. You were basically mythical creatures. Like unicorns! I never saw you until I moved to Salt Lake and planted my first garden, where I discovered you and your friends shouting "party on!" to each other beneath my leafy vegetables. Then you went ahead and ate all my leafy vegetables.

I called my father shortly after the First Great Leafy Vegetable Massacre.

"Dad," I said, "do you guys have snails down there in Provo?"

He said no. He'd never had a snail problem in his own garden. It's like there was this sign on the outskirts of town that said "Welcome to Provo. Except if you're a snail, in which case you should feel free to slither on back to Salt Lake."

So you did. You slithered on back to Salt Lake and ended up in my garden AGAIN where, in spite of my best efforts to curb your enthusiasm, you made a meal out of my hostas summer after summer after summer.

I'll admit that I tried briefly to see you through different eyes after reading *All the Light We Cannot See* last year. The heroine in that book, a young French girl named Marie-Laure, admires your kind for your ability to withstand the seabirds that try to eat you. Marie-Laure was totally Team

Snail. So I thought to myself, "Maybe snails aren't so bad after all." But then I stepped outside, saw you guys chowing your way through my garden, and realized that in the end I was (and always will be) Team Seabird.

Anyway. I was surprised when my mother told me you guys finally stepped off the bus in Provo and started helping yourself to her marigolds. Obviously this younger generation of snails is bolder than previous generations. Kids today! They're always eating other people's marigolds!

But, like I said before, the Snail Huntress is definitely after you and would appreciate any tips from a) *Trib* readers who are also b) experienced Snail Slayers. Thank you, *Trib* readers!

Meanwhile, please believe me, Snails, when I say that your days are numbered . . .

TIPTOE THROUGH THE TOMATOES WITH TINKERBELL

First Published August 2017

Dear Tinkerbell,
    Just so you know, I'm lying in wait for you. Right now. Behind the lilac bush. Early in the morning. So early, in fact, that dawn is barely cracking. Or whatever it is that dawn does early in the morning.
    I'm waiting for you to appear so I can leap to my feet and shout HA! And also GOTCHA!
    OK. Certain people reading this may wonder why I am waiting behind the lilac bush for a Disney character to appear in my backyard. Is it normal for people to do that? Is that even a thing? I need to explain, obv.
    You, Tinkerbell, are a dog—a real live Newfoundland that weighs 120 pounds, as opposed to a fake fairy who doesn't weigh anything because (as I just noted) she's fake.

When we brought you home, we figured we knew all about your kind because we owned a Newfoundland before you. Zora. We knew that you would shed and drool and sneak up on the couch because that's what Newfies do. We also knew you would adore little children, just like Katie Nana in Peter Pan.

But. There were a few things we didn't know.

Even when Zora was a puppy she was lazy. It took every last ounce of her energy to lie in the middle of the floor all day long. I once found a photo in a magazine of a Newfie leaping out of a helicopter to rescue somebody drowning in the middle of the Atlantic Ocean . . . and marveled. I knew the last thing in the world Zora wanted to do was leap out of helicopters. She barely wanted to leap out of cars. Especially when I took her to the groomer's.

So imagine our surprise, Tinkerbell, when we brought you home and discovered that leaping was one of your superpowers. You leap everywhere. Up and down staircases. On furniture. Over furniture.

But here's the thing I REALLY didn't expect, which is why I'm hiding behind the lilac bush. You have apparently developed a taste for tomatoes. Fresh ones, straight off the vine. My vines. The ones I planted with hope in my heart last May.

Yes, I thought to myself as I carefully placed those tiny tomato plants in my garden. Come August and September I will be able to enjoy the literal fruits (because tomatoes, technically speaking, are fruits and not vegetables) of my labor. I will pluck warm ripe tomatoes straight out of my garden and eat them as I sit on my back porch.

However, as the Scottish poet Robert Burns once said, "The best laid plans of mice and men often go awry." Except he said it in Scottish. "The best laid schemes o' mice an' men gang aft a-gley." Which explains why I only understood half of what I heard that time I was in Glasgow trying to order some curry in a restaurant.

Here's what happened. One morning I noticed that tomatoes were missing. Also, the plants themselves looked like Paul Bunyan had stepped on them. Paul Bunyan? What?! Later, I caught sight of you, Tinkerbell, rummaging through those same plants like someone at a garage sale.

YOU! You are Paul Bunyan. Except not really. Because he's fake, too. But that's not the point. The point is that I'm going to bust you this morning. I'm going to shoot out from behind this bush and shout, "UNHAND THOSE TOMATOES."

Which you will. And you'll look at me with big repentant brown eyes.

But as soon as my back is turned, you'll help yourself to them again.

Which leaves me no other choice but this: to plant my tomatoes in the front yard when spring rolls around once again. Live and learn, Tink. That's what this life is all about.

Tinkerbell

Here's something I'll never do again—wear my hair like this.

GETTING MY PHILSOPHY ON

Once when I was eating a chili cheese dog for lunch at the Der Wienerschnitzel across the street from Provo High School (I remember everything in my life by what I was eating at the time), my friend Debbie made this observation: "You're always talking like a philosopher or something."

I could tell she didn't mean that as a compliment.

Seriously, who wants to eat chili cheese dogs with philosophers when you're a sophomore in high school? BORING.

Still, Debbie had picked up on the tendency I have to ask what it all means.

I don't have many answers. But over the years I've written about the ideas chasing each other's tails around in my brain. A few of those columns can be found in this section.

And now I'm hungry for a chili cheese dog.

My mother believes everyone, depresed or not, should own a dog.

Thanks, Jan Sloan! This bacon ornament looks great on our Christmas tree next to the Spam ornament.

WEIGHTY MATTERS

First Published February 2014

When it comes to weighing ourselves in the morning, my husband and I take opposite approaches. Is this because he's a guy and I'm not? Or is it because we're just two different people. Maybe you can help me decide.

Here's what my husband does. He makes sure that the needle is exactly on zero. Then he stands on the scale. Boom. That's it. As far as I can tell, he doesn't feel much angst about the procedure. He just gets it done and moves on.

For me things aren't that simple. I have to weigh myself in stages.

The first stage is all about preparing to get on the scales. This involves me getting rid of anything on my person that will make me heavier. Shoes. Socks. Jewelry. Reading glasses. Fingernail polish. Fingernails. I take things right down to the lowest layer of skin possible.

After I do this, I then prepare the scale itself. While my husband always starts out with the needle right at zero, I like to begin with the needle resting a little to the left of zero. I don't exactly wander into negative number territory (look! I just used some algebra!) when I re-set the scale, but yeah. Let's just say I like to start my day off on the slim side of zilch.

The second stage of weighing is all about the approach. Whereas my husband leaps on and off the scale like a mountain goat, I proceed with caution. I slowly, slowly, slowly lift one foot onto the scale and wait until the scale settles at a number I can (sort of) live with. Then, while holding my breath, I place my hands on a nearby wall as I slowly, slowly, slowly lift my other foot and carefully place it next to its partner. Toes first. Then the ball. And finally the heel.

There. I'm on the scale now. Time for the third stage. I close my eyes and shoot a frantic prayer to the Weight Gods, hoping against hope that somehow the chocolate Dunford doughnut (followed by a chocolate Dunford doughnut chaser) I ate the night before won't register.

Then. I. Take. My. Hands. Off. The. Wall.

And open my eyes. And depending on what number I see before me, I'm either a) depressed or b) not as depressed as I could be.

Oh, trust me. I know this procedure is all kinds of stupid. It's beyond stupid, actually. And I hate that I'm this way. Why can't I just get my morning mountain goat on and spring onto a scale like my husband does?

But the truth is that the activity of weighing myself is fraught with messy emotion. Every time I step onto a scale, I still remember those long ago days when I was in a drill team where our leader made members weigh in front of each other and then shamed those of us who'd clearly eaten more than a celery stick for lunch.

And as you've probably guessed, I am not a natural-born

celery-eater. Unless, of course, there's lots of Ranch dressing involved.

So. Back to my original question. Are these contrasting reactions gender-based? Or are they experience-based? Frankly, I'm inclined to think women have more issues on this front than men do. But I could be wrong.

Just wondering.

LOSING THINGS

First Published September 2015

    Is it possible for people to change?
    I ask this question because of a realization I had the other day while looking for my gray sweater.
    But before I tell you about it, you should know that I was the kind of kid who always lost things. Library books. Lunch money. Articles of clothing. Homework. Notes from teachers. I just left myself hither and yon, coming and going, all over Utah Valley.
    About the only thing I never lost was food, because you know. It was FOOD.
    I drove my parents crazy, and unbeknownst to me at the time, they use to lay bets on whether or not I'd return home with the stuff I'd carried out the front door earlier in the day.
    Hey, thanks for the vote of confidence, Parents!
    Anyway, a few years ago I went to a psychic who told me I've had a) many previous lives and b) that I have always been the same person in all of those previous lives. She wasn't

specific, so I tried to imagine for myself what all those lives must have looked like.

PRE-HISTORIC ME: I live somewhere in central France with my husband and our three (surviving) children. None of us has teeth. But that's not the point. My husband paints cave walls for a living. He's mostly happy in his job, but sometimes he complains. "Bison, bison, bison. That's all people want me to paint these days. What I wouldn't give to paint a horse now and then." Meanwhile I have misplaced my club.

"Has anybody seen my club?" I ask.

MEDIEVAL ME: I live in a nunnery in Flanders where I spend my day doing embroidery, making lace collars for rich merchants' wives and praying—that is, when I can find my rosary.

"Has anybody seen my rosary?" I ask.

HAWAIIAN ME: I live in the islands shortly before Captain Cook shows up and ruins all the reindeer games by giving us diseases. Hey, thanks for that, Captain Cook! In spite of the diseases, this is my favorite lifetime by far because you know. SEA! SAND! SUN! Too bad I can't remember where I parked my outrigger canoe.

"Has anybody seen my canoe?" I ask.

REVOLUTIONARY WAR ME: Somehow I wind up in the American colonies, fighting against the British who want to tax my tea because you know how the British are—always taxing other people's tea whenever they feel like it. It's a dodgy dangerous lifetime, mostly because I can't find my musket.

"Has anybody seen my musket?" I ask.

PIONEER ME: I decide to trek across the plains with

the Mormons to Utah, and along the way I sing as I walk and walk and walk. I had a covered wagon at one time, which would have eliminated the necessity for all that walking. But somehow I lost my ox.

"Has anybody seen my ox?" I ask.

NEW YORK ME: It's the 1950s. I'm in a gang called the Jets. My gang likes to wear tight pants and have dance-offs with a rival gang called the Sharks. The only problem is that sometimes I can't find my tight pants.

"Has anybody seen my tight pants?" I ask.

ME ME: And now it's 2015. I'm looking through my closet for that gray sweater, half-expecting it to be gone. Because you know. I lose things. But guess what. MY GRAY SWEATER IS THERE! It's hanging up. Waiting for me.

And that's when I realized I haven't lost anything (except my mind) (but whatever) for a long time.

So. Back to our original question. Can people change?

Yes.

Even if it takes a few lifetimes to do it.

STUFF I NEVER HAVE TO DO AGAIN

First Published July 2016

    I had one of those big milestone birthdays this spring, which means yessir I am officially old now. If I get hit while crossing the street tomorrow, the newspaper headline will read: "ELDERLY WOMAN STRUCK BY A CAR."

    That's what happens if you live long enough. Newspapers start calling you an elderly woman when you get struck by cars.

    But here's the deal. There are certain distinct advantages to being this age. WHO KNEW? One of the biggest perks is this: there's a whole lotta stuff you just don't have to do anymore because guess what. You've already been there. You've already done that.

    Here are a few examples. When you're officially old you don't have to . . .

    --Get sent to the principal's office.

    --Be a den mother.

--Go to juvenile courts with one (or more) of your sons.
--Hide in a car trunk to get into a drive-in movie for free.
--Take geometry at Provo High School.
--Run for sixth-grade president and lose.
--Tell your dad you ran into a parked car on University Avenue while wearing a drill team uniform.
--Eat oatmeal for breakfast. Unless you want to. (Which I don't.)
--Wear corrective shoes.
--Play hopscotch at recess while wearing corrective shoes with your friend Cindy Eakins (who also wore corrective shoes) because no one else in the second grade would play with you guys.
--Go to Fashion Fabrics on Center Street in Provo with your mom and wait while she thumbs through a stack of Butterick pattern books. GAH! SHOOT ME!
--Wear a green one-piece gymsuit in P.E. class.
--Take a shower after P.E. class so the teachers can mark you off as one of the clean ones.
--Help your kids do a science fair project the night before the science fair.
--Sell Sally Foster giftwrap.
--Help your kids do their paper routes to teach them some more responsibility.
--Make your kids practice the piano.
--Give birth.
--Read *Moby-Dick*.
--Make your sons read *The Scarlet Letter*.
--Wear your brown polyester Taco Time uniform to work. Especially if you don't work at Taco Time anymore.
--Run a marathon. Unless you want to. (Which I don't.)
--Do the jump splits.
--Have that plate and seven screws removed from your

right wrist. (Already did it. Thanks, Dr. Huish.)

--Get a perm. Unless you want to.

--Sew a vest and an A-line skirt in Home Ec out of kettle cloth. (You were a great teacher, Mrs. Warner, but I just wasn't a very good seamstress.)

--Keep gerbils as pets.

--Go on Star Tours at Disneyland and get sick to your stomach.

--Stay to the end of a game. Or a concert. Or anything else.

--Attend that special hell otherwise known as "seventh grade."

--Weigh yourself.

--Eat dessert AFTER dinner.

--Share a room with your younger brother.

--Observe a curfew.

--Enforce a curfew.

--Go to Parent Teacher Conferences.

--Attend an elementary school maturation talk.

--Toilet train a toddler.

--Apologize to parents because your kid bit their kid at church.

--Even though their kid deserved to be bitten.

--Kidding!

--Dye your hair.

--Ask for permission.

--Care what anybody thinks.

It's not that I'm unhappy I did many of these things. I remember with special fondness, for instance, that time I went to a maturation talk with one of our sons and burst out laughing like I was a fifth-grade boy myself. But it's time to move on.

And try something new.

FLOSSING AND OTHER NEWLY DECLARED EVILS

First Published August 2016

Today I want to discuss things that used to be good/bad for us that are now bad/good for us. Does that make sense?

The first thing is the sun. Back when I was growing up, the sun was a good thing because the sun made you tan and tan = junior high school popularity. Score! This is why the girls my age basted ourselves with baby oil and then went to the swimming pool to "lay out" and broil. Also, the sun gave you sexy time blond highlights, especially if you sprayed your wet hair with Sun-In. So, see? The sun was a good thing.

But then party-pooper experts started saying that sun gave you cancer and that everybody should use sunscreen and wear burkas (including the men) whenever they went outside. The sun had become Public Enemy Number One, just sitting up there in the sky waiting to hurl thunderbolts of cancer at people. I know this from personal experience, actually, because we've had the skin cancer thing in my own family.

But now? The sun is still a bad guy. Just not as bad. In fact, the sun is more like an anti-hero—a badass with a few redeeming qualities such as being an excellent source of Vitamin D. So now experts are saying you should still wear sunscreen but leave the burkas at home.

Whole milk is another thing that used to be good for people before it was bad for people before it was good for people again. Or at least this is what my husband's running partner Paul recently said. It used to be everyone drank whole milk because whole milk came from cows and cows are our friends. Of course our friends the cows wouldn't want to hurt us or clog our arteries or make our hearts explode.

But then party-pooper experts started saying whole milk bumped up your level of cholesterol, which is why skim milk and 2% were invented, which don't taste as good but have the distinct advantage of not killing you.

Except now, according to my husband's running partner Paul, people are saying whole milk actually lowers your cholesterol. I don't know how Paul knows this, but when it comes to issues involving milk, I trust him implicitly.

Which brings me to flossing. Did you see where the government is now saying there's no correlation between flossing and preventing tooth decay? Okay. This just seems completely counterintuitive. How is possible that those poppy seeds stuck in your teeth ever since you ate that wedding cake last weekend can be a good thing? Can anybody really promise me that those poppy seeds have my teeth's best interest at heart?

Here's the deal. I came late to the flossing party, and I am reluctant to give up a hygiene habit that was hard for me to form. Why was it so hard for me to form? Because I'm lazy.

How lazy am I? Some days it's just too much effort to push the power button on my TV's remote control. Some days it's just too much effort to lift a donut to my mouth. Even a donut from Fresh Donuts and Deli on State Street. Some days it's just too hard to open a can of Dr Pepper. Some days it's just too much effort to breathe.

The sloth is my spirit animal, yo.

But when I finally climbed aboard the Flossing Express I became a believer. My gums tingled with happiness, as well as hope in a future not involving tooth decay. And now the government wants to take my floss away from me? I don't think so.

Hey! Hands off my dental floss, Government!

Go pick on someone else.

WHEN THINGS MATTER

First Published August 2014

    If you're the kind of reader who likes a story seasoned with irony, then you might appreciate this one.
    So my maternal grandmother gave me her doll a long time ago. A great big beautiful bisque girl with blue glass eyes and a mohair wig made in Germany. It was hard for my grandmother to hand over that doll—especially to me, because the sad truth is that I am as a clumsy as a bull in a china shop. Except that I'm a girl. So technically that would make me as clumsy as a cow in a china shop.
    See? When it comes to cattle trivia, I am ON IT.
    Anyway. My brother once said that he could always tell when I'd opened a cereal box because it looked like Big Foot had been in our pantry, and my husband still says my favorite tool is a hammer. You get the picture. I'm hard on things. Very, very hard on things.
    But here's the deal. Because I was her only granddaughter, my grandmother had no choice but to leave the doll with me. And I have taken excellent care of her.

She's been sitting in a tiny rocker by the fireplace where she has unnerved neighborhood children for years because (I've since been told) that antique dolls are super creepy and scary.

Sorry about that, Neighborhood Children! I had no idea I was scarring you for life! And btw I also had no idea you guys were such big weenies!

But that's not the point. The point is this–last weekend we had a huge open house, and as I was bustling about getting ready for all our guests, it occurred to me that the doll would be safer if I moved her into another room. Which I did. And sure enough, nobody at the open house accidently broke the doll. Which is why she was as lovely and pristine as ever this morning. Until I tripped over the rocker myself. And heard the sick thud of a bisque doll doing a face-plant on a hardwood floor.

As I scooped up the pieces of my grandmother's doll, my hands shaking, I told myself that things are only things. They don't matter. Like Patricia Arquette's character in the movie *Boyhood* observed, you spend the first half of your life acquiring stuff and the second half of your life getting rid of it. And I have been getting rid of stuff like crazy this summer—tearing through closets and drawers and dispatching things to D.I. like the Blues Brothers on a mission from God.

But when that doll broke this morning, I remembered my grandmother's funeral and how when we took my grandfather back to their home after the service was over, he asked us to leave him alone for awhile.

"Are you sure?" My mother asked, her brow furrowed in concern. "Wouldn't you rather come up to the house with us?"

My grandfather shook his head. "I just want to sit here for awhile. You know. With Louise's things."

And so we honored his request. We left him sitting in the home he and his wife had built together—weak wintry sunlight slanting through the window—surrounded by the artifacts of a life.

It's true what they say. Things don't matter much.

Until they do.

My grandmother's doll, terrorizing the neighborhood children since 1985.

I WISH YOU MORE

First Published August 2015

    If you could wish someone you love more of something (anything!), what would it be?
    That's the question Amy Krouse Rosenthal and Tom Lichtenheld consider in their new children's picture book, *I Wish You More*. Some of their responses include the following.
    "I wish you more ups than downs."
    "I wish you more give than take."
    "I wish you more we than me."
    "I wish you more pause than fast-forward."
    "I wish you more bubbles than bath."
    It's a charming little book, and after I read it I tried to come up with a few of my own wishes, following the same pattern. Here they are, with my editorial notes included.
    I wish you more understanding than misunderstandings. [Hmmm. Possible cliche?]
    I wish you more roses than aphids. [Aphids! Ew!]
    I wish you more listening than talking. [Whatever. I like

to talk.]

I wish you more Fridays than Mondays. [SCORE!]

I wish you more downhills than uphills. [Wait. Does that sound too much like the "more ups than downs" thing?]

I wish you more summers than winters. [Yeah! That's what I'm talking about.]

I wish you more dancing than sitting. [Except if you have bad knees.]

I wish you more doughnuts than not doughnuts. [Now you're just being an idiot.]

Fine. But I still wish you more doughnuts than not doughnuts. [OK. We're done here.]

I know. I'm super lame. But the point is I've been thinking about wishes for the people we love because my husband and I have a son getting married this weekend. Our baby, in fact. [HOW DID THIS HAPPEN? Didn't I just register that baby boy for kindergarten? Which means I have a child in kindergarten who's getting married? Is that even legal?]

Except.

He's not in kindergarten anymore.

He's a man now. A shining bright big-hearted man. He turned into one while I turned my back for a few minutes. And he's marrying a splendid young woman who's just right for him. And so I will wish for this couple the things my grandmother wished for my husband and me the day we were married.

For the record, I know I'm repeating myself here—I've written columns about her toast before, including her little joke that she'd never toasted a bride before, so she hoped she wouldn't "burn" me. But whenever I read her handwritten notes, which I keep in a small wooden box by my bed, I think of my grandmother standing at the head of a table and saying these words in a voice full of years.

    May you have ...
Enough happiness to make you sweet;
Enough trials to keep you strong;
Enough sorrow to keep you human;
Enough hope to keep you happy;
Enough failure to keep you humble;
Enough success to keep you eager;
Enough friends to give you comfort;
Enough faith in yourself to give you courage;
Enough wealth to meet your needs;
And enough determination to make each day a good day.

    These are my wishes, too, for my son and his bride. I want them to have the all of it—joy and sorrow and failure and success and plenty of grit. But most of all I wish them love.

    And then more love.

DEAR BACON

First Published November 2015

Dear Bacon,

    Is it true what The World Health Organization says about you? That you'll give me cancer if I don't quit you? I think the WHO is serious about their claims, too. According to a recent NPR report, they're putting you in the same category as asbestos and smoking. SMOKING! Who knew? So instead of cutting class and sneaking a smoke in the bathroom or the high school parking lot, rebellious teenagers all across America can just eat some bacon instead?

    Oh, Bacon. You're the bad boy of the food world these days. You might as well just slick your hair back, put on a white T-shirt and a Levi jacket a la James Dean, and throw smoldering glances from the driver's seat of your El Camino at all the girls who walk by. They'll have a hard time resisting you, of course, even though their mothers (as well as the World Health Organization) will tell them not to get involved with you.

    "Bacon will break your heart!" They'll say. "And also

clog your arteries! Who needs a boyfriend that clogs your arteries?"

Answer: Me, apparently.

Bacon, I fell under your bad-boy spell years ago. Like, when I was in kindergarten. To me, you were the best part of every breakfast. Certainly better than oatmeal. Even better than the silver dollar pancakes my friend's dad used to make at slumber parties. He was famous for his pancakes that were the size of—wait for it!—silver dollars. And he always instigated a competition to see who could eat the most.

"Hey, girls!" he'd say. "Who can eat the most?"

I won. Always. And then I was rewarded with more pancakes.

But, Bacon, I would have preferred to have YOU as my reward. Anytime. All the time.

I still feel that way, too. And I don't just like you for breakfast. I like you in my sandwiches and soups. I like you sprinkled on top of my salads and baked potatoes. I like you wrapped (lovingly) (like an embrace) around my meat loaf.

I also like you for dessert.

The first time I ever flew into Eugene, Oregon to visit my son and his wife, we did not pass "Go," we did not collect $200.00 when they picked me up at the airport. Instead, they drove me straight to Voodoo Doughnut where we ordered Bacon Maple Bars. I've since sampled maple bacon doughnuts from other establishments, but none has compared to that first sublime introduction.

(And speaking of desserts, I also like chocolate-covered bacon. As if that even needed to be said, duh.)

But whatever. That's not the point. The point is that you're a bad boyfriend, Bacon, and I need to quit you. But can I? I have the feeling that even after I send you packing in your El Camino, I'll still be stalking you online, seeing what you're up to. And every time you update your status as a key ingredient in everything from bacon jam to bacon-wrapped dates stuffed with cream cheese to Brie and bacon pasta (with basil!) to bacon and cheddar scones, my heart will break a little.

That's right, Bacon. Our mothers were right about you. And they would know.

Because our mothers loved you, too.

Sincerely,

Ann Cannon

THIS I BELIEVE

First Published January 2015

    My friend Louise and I were talking about the concept of belief the other day, which made me think about the ongoing This I Believe project (http://thisibelieve.org) where ordinary people write essays outlining their core values. So I decided to make a list of my own beliefs, which looks something like this.

    I believe that depressed people should own a dog.

    I believe that everybody should plant at least one tomato plant every spring, even if they never succeed in getting tomatoes. It's a hopeful thing to do.

    I believe that kindness is a more admirable personality trait than intelligence.

    And speaking of intelligence, I believe it comes in all shapes and sizes.

    I believe that status and rank are overrated and that whenever possible, we should politely ignore them.

    I believe you can tell a lot about a person by the way he treats the people who can't do anything for him.

I believe that exercise is good for the body and even better for the soul.

I believe that having low expectations actually increases your level of happiness in this life.

I believe that football as we know it will no long exist 50 years from now.

I believe that would make me sad—if I were still around to watch a game.

I believe in having a pile of books by my bedside at all times, even if I never get around to reading them all.

I believe that there are no easy solutions to the country's big problems. Same goes for the world's problems, and anybody who tells you differently has a crate of snake oil in the trunk of his Cadillac.

I believe the good things about people can also be the challenging things about them.

I believe a woman should be able to do whatever she wants to with her hair.

I believe a person should spend as much time outside as possible.

I believe an individual should not be denied opportunity based on gender or race.

I believe that compromise is not a dirty word.

I believe that there is more than one way to skin a cat.

Not that I believe in skinning cats.

I believe that no matter how old you get, you need people in your life who remember the same music, the same movies, the same current events that you do. You need your peers.

I believe children should be given space without constant adult direction.

I believe money spent on a good meal in a restaurant is never money wasted.

I believe, if possible, you should find a way to keep

talking to your siblings.

I believe that associating only with people who see the world the same way you do leads to myopia.

I believe that travel—even if you don't travel far from home—creates its own kind of literacy.

Where politicians are concerned I DEFINITELY believe in an aggressive press.

I believe all people are hypocrites in one way or another, so we should all cut each other a little slack.

I believe people should discover what they're good at doing and then do it.

I believe it's stupid to take offense. Most people don't mean to offend, and even if they do, why give them power over you?

I believe that the experience of failing is often more valuable than the experience of succeeding.

I believe that things could be worse and they probably will be, so why not find something about your present situation to enjoy?

I believe you should take care of your family and remain loyal to your friends.

And finally, I believe that shoes should be comfortable and pants should be stretchy.

Here's something else I believe. You're never too old to (almost) sit on Santa's lap.

My men playing a pickup game. From left to right: Dylan, Ken, Phil, Quinton, Geoff and Alec

SPORTS AND THE WHOLE NINE YARDS!

Sports played an important part in shaping what our family's life looked like. My father, LaVell Edwards, was a football coach, so yes. Sports mattered.

Would I have been a fan if I'd grown up in another family? Seriously, I don't know. That's like asking if W. would have thought about running for president if his dad, George H., hadn't already done the same thing. Sports were just a part of our family's landscape.

Meanwhile, I grew up and married a man who wrote a master's thesis about baseball in territorial Utah. We proceeded to have five sons together, thus ensuring that sports, in one form or another, would remain a part of my life.

I'm a fan and I own it.

This section features columns about baseball and football. But mostly baseball.

Showing some Cub love, Christmas 2016

Yikes! How did I wind up wearing a University of Utah blanket?

HEY CHICAGO, WHADDYA SAY!

First Published October 2016

For Mike Royko:
Today I'm going to discuss what can happen if you finally get that thing you've always wanted. But first, a little backstory.

Okay. Even if you don't follow baseball you've probably heard by now that the Chicago Cubs clinched the pennant Saturday night. This is a BIG DEAL because the Cubs, who were once cursed by a goat that was banned from Wrigley Field (and you know how are goats are when you start banning them from ballparks), haven't won a pennant since man discovered fire.

So yeah. There was euphoria all around when the Cubs took down the best pitcher in baseball (Kershaw) and smacked the Dodgers' little behinds, thus catapulting the team (the Cubs, not the Dodgers) into the World Series. That euphoria extended all the way out here to Utah where some of the Cannons began weeping with joy.

People sometimes ask why we're Cubs fans. After all, we're not from Illinois, although we have driven through Illinois several times, once with a large U-Haul and three cocker spaniels. No. We're Cubs fans because of the Summer of the Yellow Eyeballs.

It all started when I noticed that our son Alec, who was 5 years old at the time, was turning a different color. When I took him to the doctor, the doctor said Alec was turning a different color because he was eating too many carrots. I thought this was odd because of all the things I'd seen Alec eat too much of, carrots were not on the top of the list. But whatever. Doctors are smart, so I figured he must have been right.

Except my mom wasn't having any of it. "Your doctor's an idiot," she said. And my mom, as she often is, was right. Within hours everybody in our family had changed colors. Especially our eyeballs. Which were yellow. That's what happens when you all contract a mysterious case of viral hepatitis.

Anyway. I spent much of that summer in bed because that's what happens when you contract a mysterious case of viral hepatitis AND you are also pregnant. Meanwhile the TV got stuck on WGN, and because both my husband and I were too tired to change the channel (hepatitis makes you too tired to change channels FYI) we watched the Cubs play ball all summer long.

The Cubs became our best friends. Andre Dawson. Shawon Dunston. Ryne Sandberg. Vance Law. Doug Dascenzo. Rick Sutcliffe. Those guys would have totally brought us get-better-soon casseroles if only they'd lived in Salt Lake City and not Chicago.

Even after we got better the Cubs remained our

best friends, because, as it turns out, we have the right temperament to be Cubs fans. We are the kind of people who are always expecting the other shoe to drop, which is the main requirement if you sign up to be a Cubs fan. You must believe that things could be worse and they probably will be. You must have a taste for the sound of your own heart breaking. You must be able to laugh (mirthlessly if necessary) whenever you hear that joke about how any team can have an off-century. You must nod in agreement when you remember the advice the great late columnist Mike Royko once shared with his readers: Mamas, don't let your babies grow up to be Cubs fans.

So what do fans like us do when—surprise!—our team IS ACTUALLY PLAYING IN THE WORLD SERIES?

Does the ground shift beneath our feet? Do we double-down on our decades-long angst? Are we poised to experience a massive identity crisis?

Oh, hell no.

We're gonna buckle up and enjoy this ride for as long as it lasts.

(Maybe.)

THIRTY THINGS I LEARNED WHILE RUNNING THE ST. GEORGE MARATHON LAST WEEKEND

First Published October 2012

1. St. George knows how to throw a first-rate party for runners. A HUGE high five for everyone involved (with a special thanks to Robert Snow). Three words describe the event: awesome, awesome, and awesome.
2. Running a marathon, oddly, is a lot like writing a novel. The middle part is the hardest.
3. It does not hurt to have an iPod loaded with B.B. King tunes. (Favorite lyric? "I let you live in my penthouse, you said it was just a shack. I gave you seven children and now you want to give them back.")

4. Speaking of which, how did people run marathons before iPods were invented?
5. (BTW, I was the nutball singing along to "Viva Las Vegas" somewhere near Mile 19.)
6. People who cheer you on—even if they don't know you—make a big difference.
7. People who cheer you on—even if they DO know you—make a big difference, too. (Thanks, Ken and Geoff. Thanks, Kim. Thanks, Mom and Dad.)
8. Running 26.2 miles is as challenging mentally as it is physically.
9. Still, it is totally, totally worth running that distance just to hear your teenage son say, "My mom is badass."
10. You should look past the finish line when running the last four blocks. Otherwise the sight of it—so near, yet so far away—will make you crazy.
11. Guys and their special guy "plumbing" have a distinct advantage over women on a long run.
12. Running a marathon is hard. But giving birth is harder.
13. I liked the advice given to me on the bus ride up the canyon by a woman who has run a number of marathons. "Enjoy every minute of your run—the good, the bad, and the ugly. And remember that the ugly always makes for a better story."
14. When this same woman discovered I was a first-time marathoner, she predicted I would be planning my next marathon as soon as I crossed the finish line.
15. She was wrong.
16. The bonfires at the race's starting line were a nice touch.
17. Same for the cold wet towels at the race's end.
18. Is drinking milk right after a long race actually good for you? I seriously want to know, so please advise.
19. The race does, in fact, go to the swift. And to the non-

swift, too.

20. People have asked why I wanted to run a marathon in the first place, because running that far is crazy. I had my reasons, including this: I want my kids to know that I can do hard things. And they can, too.

21. Even though in the interest of full disclosure I also had to tell them I finished in the bottom 10%.

22. BUT COME ON, DUDES! I finished! And not on a stretcher!

23. However, I do think it's possible I was under-prepared for the experience.

24. But then I am always under-prepared.

25. For everything.

26. Which is why everything in life always takes me by surprise! Like that hill at Mile Seven.

27. One of my favorite sights? A guy running shirtless with the words JUST MARRIED scrawled across his back like he was a human rear window.

28. As it turns out, running the actual marathon is easier than training for it.

29. But still. It's obvious I ain't 23 years old anymore.

30. Thank goodness!

GRANDCHILDREN AT THE BALLPARK

First Published August 2016

    Last weekend my husband and I took two of our grandchildren (a 6-year-old girl and a 2-year-old boy) to a Bees game, which taught me this interesting life lesson. You treat your grandkids a whole lot differently at a baseball game than you treated your own kids.

    For example!

    When your own kids asked if they could have cotton candy at the ballpark you said, "No. It'll spoil your dinner."

    Or you said, "No. It's too expensive."

    Or you said, "No. It'll rot out all those teeth in your head."

    Or you said, "No. Cotton candy is disgusting."

    And if you DID break down and buy your own kids cotton candy, you said, "Ugh. The cotton candy goes in your mouth, not all over you face."

    Or you said, "Ugh. That was a total waste of money."

Or you said, "Ugh. DON'T TOUCH ME, YOU GUYS."

But if your grandkids ask for cotton candy, you say, "Of course!" And then you snap your fingers at the cotton candy garcon (he's the guy carrying stuff on a stick up and down the aisles) and tell him to bring you a bag or two of his finest, after which you hand the cotton candy over to the grandkids who don't put it in their mouths either, but for some reason you find this charming instead of maddening.

You find it so charming, in fact, that you take pictures with your smartphone and post them on Facebook, so that all the other grandparents on Facebook will see just how charming your grandchildren with cotton candy smeared on their faces (and possibly in their hair) really are.

It's the same with the kiddy train at the Bees game. Basically you have to wait an hour to take a five-minute ride. And if your kids are really young, you have to ride with them in the train yourself, at which time you discover there is no room for your knees.

So there's that.

Which is why you said, "There's no room for my knees in the train" when your own kids asked if they could go for a ride.

Or you said, " The line's too long.

Or you said, "It's too hot and also the line's too long."

Or you said, "Our family doesn't believe in train rides."

But if your grandkids ask for a train ride, you say, "Of course! Who needs knees anyway?" And you happily stand in a long line while they smear cotton candy in each other's hair, after which you crawl into a train car (all scrunched up like Harry Houdini) and wave at strangers as the train putts around the south end of the ballpark.

Okay. I just read what I've written so far, and now I'm wondering if I was a bad mother—or if not exactly a bad mother, at least a grumpypants mother. I don't know. You'll have to ask my kids.

I do know this, though. When I was the mother of young children, I was tired all the time. Really, really tired. Raising young children is so much about physical maintenance—feeding them, clothing them, cleaning up after them, and keeping them safe. There's more, too—reminding them to finish their homework or do their chores or return their library books or walk the dog they promised to walk faithfully before you bought it or play nice even when they don't want to.

You're in the trenches with your own kids.

But with your grandkids? Not so much.

So, yeah. Bring on the cotton candy. And. Do. Not. Skimp.

MEDITATION WHILE WATCHING A GRAND-DAUGHTER (SORT OF) PLAYING SOCCER

First Published October 2014

When you're young you think a lot about the future. Where will you live? Who will you marry? How many kids will you have? What will you be when you grow up? (I wanted to be something practical. Like a spy. Or an astronaut. And when I was in the second grade, I wanted to be "Miss Arizona" in the Miss America Beauty Pageant, even though I was from Utah. I just thought Arizona was awesome because everybody had a swimming pool there.)

When you're not young, you think a lot about the past.

This can be pleasant sometimes—especially when you remember the good times you had with family and friends. But thinking about the past can be troubling, too. Lately

I've been examining my years as a young mother. Who knows why? It's not like I can crawl into Christopher Lloyd's Delorean and change the things that have already happened.

Still. I find myself wondering about the things I did and didn't do.

Why didn't I read to them every night, for example?

And why did I let them quit the piano and violin?

Why wasn't I better about making them take their fluoride pills each morning?

And why did we eat so much macaroni and cheese? The kind you make from a box?

Okay. I'll stop because this kind of thinking is so pointless, NOT TO MENTION BORING. My kids are all grown up now, and in spite of my many failings as a parent, they're doing just fine on their own. But seriously? Why did I let so many things—important things, even—fall through the cracks?

And this, my friends, is why you should have grandchildren.

Case in point. My granddaughter is playing soccer for the first time this fall, and she isn't loving it. In fact, when I watched her play on Saturday, she spent a lot of time sitting on the sidelines, crying.

I thought she looked pretty cute, actually, in her cute little uniform and her cute little pink cleats with cute little tears streaming down her cute little face. She was so cute, in fact, that I started to laugh. Hahahahahahaha! Which only made her cry some more.

Her parents, on the other hand, were a little frustrated, and who can blame them? Who knew there was crying in soccer?

Here's the deal. Everything about raising kids looks so manageable on paper, right? You sign up for soccer. Check!

You buy shin guards and cleats. Check! You show your kid how to kick a ball. Check! You go to the game and everybody has fun. Double check! And also scooooooore!

But what you never see on paper is the part where you can't find the shin guards on Saturday morning because the dog carried them off. Or the part where your kid would rather stay home to watch cartoons than kick a ball. Or the part where he or she sits on the sidelines and cries because someone got up on the wrong side of the bed.

Watching your grandchildren grow up reminds you of all that. It also increases the respect you feel for their young parents and helps you cut yourself a little bit of slack.

Whenever you start looking backwards.

THAT WAS THEN, THIS IS NOW

First Published January 2013

    See that right there?
    It's a medal. In fact, it's the mother of all medals. It is the world's biggest mother of all medals. Also the heaviest.
    How heavy is it, you ask? SO heavy that if you pick it up, your arm will automatically fall off. That's right. If it were any heavier, both of your arms would automatically fall off. It's a medal so heavy that mere arms cannot hold it. And guess what. It's mine. ALL MINE!
    I know, right?
I received it after running a half-marathon last weekend with my daughter-in-law. I came in 3151st place. Yes, you read that correctly. 3151st place. Yay! Go, Me!
    Okay, fine. I lied. Not about the 3151st place part. About the medal part. It's probably not the world's biggest medal. Maybe Muhammad Ali has a bigger one. Who knows? Who cares? Certainly not me. My medal is plenty

big and I love it and I am wearing it everywhere I go (even to weddings and funerals) for the rest of my life.

Why am I so proud of it? I'm not sure, but it might have something to do with the fact that I grew up in the days before Title IX, and thus my opportunities to snag huge honking medals for participating in organized sports were limited.

It's not like there weren't teams out there for women before Title IX. Old-timers will remember the Shamrocks. My aunt played softball when she was in the Navy during WWII. Girls played on church teams. And of course there were plenty of secondary schools around the country with strong athletic programs for young women.

But my high school wasn't one of them. Unless you were super athletic (in which case you were involved with GAA) there wasn't a lot going on for average girls like me. You tried out for the drill team, not the tennis team. In fact, there wasn't a tennis team for girls, which is why a talented classmate of mine had to play with the boys. Her story even made the local news. Imagine! A girl good enough to play with the boys!

Fortunately things have changed. I realized this after watching a baseball game many years ago with one of our young sons, who asked what position I'd played when I was a kid. I explained to him that I hadn't played on a team when I was his age.

"Why?" he asked, truly surprised. He knew, after all, how much I enjoy watching baseball.

"Because I was a girl."

"So?"

"Girls didn't play."

From the look on his face, you would have thought I'd told him I grew up in a cave and rode a brontosaurus to the grocery store whenever my mom needed a gallon of milk.

"Well that's stupid," he said, appalled.

His response was heartening. Here was a boy who simply could not conceive of a time when little girls couldn't play on a team—just because they were little girls.

And that's why I like my medal. I'm catching up, don't you know. And then one day I hope I'm so indifferent to all my medals and trophies that I can put them in a dusty box and send them out to DI when it's time to move on.

Just like boys—and girls!—do now.

HOW TO MAKE YOUR BUTT LOOK BIG

First Published April 2013

MEMO TO MY PARENTS: DON'T READ THIS COLUMN.

    I had to get that out of the way before I start, because although the three of us are now old enough to order off the senior menu when we have breakfast together at the IHOP, my parents still think I am the same 16-year-old girl who broadsided our neighbor's VW. And ran into the back of a parked car in front of the football stadium. And collected speeding tickets like some kids collect bubble gum wrappers. And high-centered the family vehicle in a parking lot. And was involved in a notorious incident at Provo High School wherein a car jumped a curb and took out a sapling tree (although it must be noted that my friend Gigi Ballif was the one driving at the time).

    In fact, the only times I ever saw my granite-faced father come unglued were the times when he was my passenger.

Dude was afraid whenever I took the wheel.

Very, very afraid.

Possibly because I did stuff like suddenly slam on the brakes in the middle of an intersection, thus pitching him and a thousand returnable glass Tab bottles (we were on the way to the grocery store for my mother) into the windshield. Even a strong man cannot be expected to get over something like that quickly.

Or ever.

So. Anyway. Now that my parents aren't reading this (automobiles + me = anxiety issues for them), I can tell you what I did last Saturday. I rode in a NASCAR at the Las Vegas Motor Speedway. It's true! I did! And I did it strictly so I could write one of those columns wherein I tell you 30 things I learned from the experience. See how much I love you? I did 160 mph around a racetrack three times JUST FOR YOU.

And as I waited for my turn, I started making up a list that included the following:

1. Wearing a NASCAR jumpsuit does not automatically make you look like Danica Patrick.

2. Although wearing a NASCAR jumpsuit does automatically make your butt look bigger.

HOWEVER. The longer I waited, the less able I was able to think of all the important life lessons I was learning. In fact, the longer I waited, the less able I was able to think. Period. That's because fear was taking over my brain in much the same way that the Borg assimilates alien species and renders them powerless. "Resistance is futile," Fear said to my brain, which caused my brain to run up a white flag and surrender immediately.

Seriously, what had I been thinking when I told my

husband to sign me up for a NASCAR ride? Didn't I realize how fast those cars go in real life? Also, there are no doors on NASCAR cars. Did you know? Which means you and your big old non-Danica Patrick, NASCAR jumpsuit-clad butt have to crawl through the car window. Which is not an easy feat for people like me who order the Senior Sampler off the senior menu at IHOP.

But okay. Fine. I said I'd do it, and because I am a person of my word (and also because people were watching), I did it. I buckled up and put my life in the gnarly hands of my driver, Don the Ragin' Cajun. (See photo of me and Don the Ragin' Cajun before taking off. I'm the one with the worried expression.)

And guess what? The ride was awesome! I felt just like Top Gun pulling g's. So when the ride was over I said to Don the R. C. "That was awesome!" to which Don the R. C. responded, "I can't hear you." So then I said, "THAT WAS AWESOME!" to which Don the R.C. responded, "I CAN'T HEAR YOU."

So yeah. That's something I learned right there—driving NASCAR cars for a living probably doesn't do good things for your hearing.

And here's the other thing I learned. Or re-learned. Anticipating an event is almost always worse than the event itself.

You're welcome.

Me with Don, aka the Ragin' Cajun.

Members of the Farrer Jr. High School "Marching Group" getting ready to march in the BYU Homecoming Parade. In aprons. That's Gigi on the left, Von in the middle, and me clutching my skirt.

A UTAH COUNTY GIRL AM I, SIR

When my husband and I first moved to Salt Lake City in the early 1980s, everyone asked us where we'd gone to high school. Turns out that "Provo High" isn't the right answer. At least not in Salt Lake. But whenever I head east on 800 North, lined with the memories of orchards past, and I see sunlight glinting off Squaw Peak, I still think Utah Valley is one of the prettiest places on earth. With its mountains to the east and a lake to the west, I'm glad I grew up there.

This section features columns inspired by some of the people and places I knew while growing up.

Photobombing a peach tree.

Photobombing a home perm.

DEAR T.S. ELIOT

First Published August 2012

Dear T.S. Eliot,
 Now that school's back in session, I've found myself thinking about the first time I met my high school English teacher Miss Nelson, who died the day before I left for England. I'll be honest. It wasn't love at first sight.
 I was looking forward to another year with the fabulous Mrs. DeHart, but when my friends and I walked into the classroom on the first day of school we found someone else sitting at Mrs. DeHart's desk.
 She was decidedly flamboyant-looking, this new person. Her hair was big and honey blond—not true English teacher hair, which (I thought) should be a reassuring shade of New England pewter. Like Mrs. DeHart's, for example.
 Maybe this new person was a substitute?
 But, alas—no. As soon as the bell rang, Miss Nelson stood before the class with supreme confidence and let us know that she was the new A.P. English teacher in town. I slumped down in my desk and shot her poisonous looks for

not being Mrs. DeHart.

I am notoriously stubborn, but Miss Nelson managed to wear down my ill will within a matter of weeks. Before long class felt like the best kind of dinner party where guests are expected to bring their smartest, wittiest selves to the table. Meanwhile, she was the glittering hostess who presided over us all.

How did Miss Nelson pull that off? I've been a teacher on and off for years now, and I still don't know she did it.

I do know, though, that she had a talent for guiding students through certain murky waters. Like your poetry, for example.

Okay fine, Mr. T.S. Eliot. We all got that you were a genius, a major player on the 20th century literary stage. However, please try to imagine yourself for a moment as an ordinary, hormonal American 17-year-old high school student assigned to read one of your own poems—"The Love Song of J. Alfred Prufrock," for example. COME ON! What's a kid like that supposed to do with lines like these: "I should have been a pair of ragged claws/ scuttling across the floors of silent seas."

Easy for YOU to say, Mr. T. Smartypants Eliot.

And yet as Miss Nelson asked us all the right questions, an unforgettable portrait of middle-aged disappointment began to emerge. We, her students, met a man, (your character J. Alfred) who has measured out his life "with coffee spoons," who yearns for some kind of glorious deliverance from his own mediocrity, only to spend his days wrestling with the most mundane of questions: "Shall I part my hair behind? Do I dare to eat a peach?"

And even though we students were frankly appalled by Prufrock's maddening passivity and self-pity, still we responded with a sort of adolescent empathy to his sorrowful conclusion that there will be no transforming magic in his life: "I have heard the mermaids singing, each to each," says Prufrock at the water's edge, "I do not think they will sing to me."

Ever since that day in Miss Nelson's class I have loved this brittle melancholy poem, and I have loved brittle, melancholy you, too. You, T. S. Eliot, were a gift to me from a good and generous woman.

She made a difference. Oh, such a difference!

RIP, Joyce Nelson. Teacher.

Your fan,
Ann Cannon

GIANT RABBIT

First Published September 2014

    Every morning when my husband and I walk our dogs, we see kids on their way to Wasatch Elementary, which causes me to reflect on all the ways their school experience must be different than mine was.

    For one thing today's parents walk their kids to school, which is something you never saw when I was growing up. Parents in those days just shoved you out the front door and said, "See you tonight. IF YOU COME HOME ALIVE."

    Which, surprisingly, we often did.

    Discipline was a whole different matter as well. I'm not sure how teachers punish students now—or if the word "punish" is even used these days. But I'm pretty sure they don't swat kids with rulers like my third-grade teacher did or practice Extreme Shaming like my fifth-grade teacher did.

    Seriously, my fifth-grade teacher was a master in the art of Extreme Shaming. He'd wash your mouth out with soap, put chewing gum on your nose and wind it around your ears, and smack your little behind with a frat boy paddleboard if you got out of line–which, apparently, I did a lot, because I was often on the receiving end of all those punishments.

Finally, in a fit of pique, my fifth-grade teacher told me that I had to spend the rest of the week down in the kindergarten room and do everything the kindergarteners did because OBVIOUSLY I was not mature enough to be a fifth-grader. So I packed up my pencil box and joined the little kids down the hall.

It's true that I felt foolish at first, especially since the kindergarten teacher kept giving me the Stink Eye. It was clear she wasn't going to treat me like I was Laura Ingalls Wilder and tell me to help the young'uns do their math sums. Nope. As far as she was concerned, I was one of the young'uns. A young'un that needed to be learned a lesson!

So that's why I ate graham crackers and milk and took a tiny nap on a tiny rug and colored pictures with big fat Crayola crayons and went out to baby recess with all my kindergartener classmates.

But here's the deal. It was kind of fun. A lot more fun than fifth-grade story problems, for example, that asked stuff like "how many 2-foot, 4-inch steps will a man take when walking 21.4 miles?" to which I would answer, "why doesn't he just take his car instead?"

And then on Friday came the best activity of all. The show-and-tell.

I saw all kinds of great stuff, but the best thing of all was this pet rabbit that one of the boys brought to school. I'm not kidding when I say this rabbit was as big as a pit bull. A pure white pit bull. With red eyeballs and big old pit bull muscles that rippled every time it twitched its nose. Clearly this rabbit was into some kind of illegal rabbit blood-doping regimen because everything about it was too much, too much, including the fact that it only had one ear.

It's true. This rabbit only had one ear growing straight out of the top of its head, not unlike a Kansas cornstalk in September.

My fellow kindergarten classmates and I were thunderstruck. Who even knew there were rabbits like this in the world?

Well, we did. The kindergarteners. And I counted myself lucky to be among their select number. I've never forgotten that day.

And here's something else I've never forgotten either—that punishments, even if they match the crime, do not always have the desired effect.

HOME PERMS

First Published August 2015

    My mom called the other day with the following question: "Do you think anybody in the family will want another home permanent?"

    Her question gave me pause. Are home permanents even still a thing?

    They were definitely a thing when I was growing up. My mom, who must have been a hairdresser in a previous life, had no peer when it came to giving home permanents. She'd plunk me down in a kitchen chair, whip a plastic cape around my neck, and go all Toni on me—wrapping my hair up in rods and soaking it with chemicals, after which she'd wash my hair and then put me in a closet for a few days until I stopped smelling bad.

    Kidding!

    I actually smelled bad FOR MONTHS after a typical home perm. But then so did everybody else at school whose mothers gave them home perms, too. (And, also, let me be very clear about this: my mother never put me in a closet.

She was totally progressive that way.)

My mother not only gave me perms, but she gave my brothers perms, too. Yes! I had brothers with perms! Because that's what young white males who wanted to look super bad did in the '70s. They asked their mothers to give them home perms.

Anyway. The '60s and the '70s were the Glory Days of Home Hair Processing at our house. My mother took care of us and also many of our neighbors with her mad perming skills during those decades. She continued perming hair in the years that followed—just not as frequently. (She also bleached her grandsons' hair so they went around looking like Eminem for a few years. But that's another story.)

And then one day people stopped asking for perms. So my mother bagged up the curlers and put them in the garage where they Rested in Peace until the other day when she called.

"Why do you ask?" I said.

She told me she'd been reading a book called *The Life-Changing Magic of Tidying Up: the Japanese Art of Decluttering and Organizing* by Marie Kondo. Among other things, the book recommends keeping only the things you really love and getting rid of the rest. Which (I think) is excellent advice.

Did my mother love those curlers? No. Would she ever again? Unlikely.

So I told her to go ahead and get rid of them for good.

Here's what surprised me, though. I felt a tiny (very tiny) pang when I said that—sort of like the tiny pang I felt when my parents recently announced they'd gotten rid of their landline because they're all about their fancy smartphones now.

What? You mean that phone number we'd had since

I was 11 years old? The one I called when I needed a ride home from school? Or to tell my mom I was at Gigi Ballif's house? Or to warn my dad that I'd run into the back of a parked car on University Avenue?

That old landline phone number is gone now—to that great big phonebook in the sky.

Okay. I'm being an idiot. And I want you to know that I totally stopped with the tiny pang thing after, like, two seconds because COME ON.

Still, sometimes letting go of something familiar reminds you that another chapter in your life has come to a close. But here's the good news: my hair's gonna smell great in all the chapters to follow.

(Win!)

LOVING THE PLACE WHERE YOU'VE ALWAYS BEEN

First Published August 2017

    I'm going to start off here with two tiny stories.
    First tiny story: When our second son was attending USU, one of his professors stopped in the middle of a lecture and said, "I can tell you guys are all from Utah because when you step outside you don't fall down and DIE WHENEVER YOU LOOK AT THESE AMAZING MOUNTAINS." He was from New York City where amazing mountains are not a common feature.
    (Author's note: I just checked in with my son about this story who said that the professor was actually from Chicago. Not New York. And that he didn't talk about students dying. He just said people who grow up here don't always appreciate our state's natural beauty. Frankly, I like my version of the story better, but fine. Whatever. I disclose this information

just to establish my credibility as a member of the non-fake news media.)

Second tiny story: A few years ago I drove my friend Wendy (who IS from New York City, not Chicago) to Moab. Somewhere between Price and Green River, she went a little slack-jawed and said in a voice that can only be described as reverent, "So THIS is the American West." And, unimpressed with the landscape I've seen all my life, I went yeah. It is.

I've been thinking about both of these incidents because of an experience I had on Monday with my friend Doni.

Ok. I have to interrupt myself to say that everybody needs a Doni in her life. Want someone to plan a trip bicycling across Holland and Belgium? Doni's your girl. Want someone to plan a trip walking from the east coast to the west coast in northern England? Doni's also your girl. We've known each other since we were 13 years old, and I'm lucky to still have her in my life.

Anyway. This time the big adventure was all about ziplining at Sundance, a place I haven't visited recently, which is strange because I spent a lot of time there when I was a kid. In fact, I remember Sundance before Sundance was Sundance. I remember when it was Timp Haven, a mom-and-pop ski resort with a tubing hill, a rope tow, a Poma lift, and a lodge where you could buy thick hot bread slathered with honey butter. We rode the school bus up the canyon and skied there in our lace-up boots, wooden skis and Miller bindings. Those were the days when average Americans could afford the sport.

I was thinking about all these things as I drove up Provo Canyon, when I noticed the sun glinting off the river's back and wow. The sight of it slapped me wide open. I felt like I was seeing that familiar river for the very first time.

My sense of wonder only deepened the farther up the

canyon I drove. The dappled light. The twisted scrub oaks with their thick serrated leaves. The rough, caramel-colored rocks. The wildflowers beginning to show. By the time I met up with Doni at the Sundance ticket office I was practically teary.

Yes, I thought. This. This is the American West.

When I was younger I wanted to be from somewhere else. England, preferably, where people opened their presents on Christmas Eve instead of Christmas morning and everybody talked like Haley Mills.

(Incidentally, I used to tell my second-grade classmates that I was from England and then I talked to them in a fake British Haley Mills accent.)

(NOTE TO SECOND GRADERS: Don't do this. It's annoying and it makes everybody hate you.)

So what's my point? Sometimes it takes years, decades, to realize how much you love the place where you've always been.

Here's to you, Utah.

SNOW DAY

First Published November 2010

Sunday night my 17-year-old son went to bed feeling pretty certain that Monday would be a "snow day." We were buried beneath layers of the white stuff here in the Avenues, and the storm showed no signs of stopping. (Also, we had some corn for popping.) (Also, the lights were turned way down low.) (Also, let it snow, let it snow, let it snow.)

"Dude," I told him, "prepare to be disappointed. This is Utah, not the greater D. C. metropolitan area. We don't do snow days here, although apparently we're willing to shut the whole town down for a fake Blizzard-of-the-Century these days."

Speaking of which, I entertained myself after the Storm of 2010 that Wasn't by writing headlines describing the event: "BLIZZARD SCHMIZZARD" or "THE BLIZZ THAT FIZZED."

My son wasn't convinced about the snow day thing, however. And he still wasn't convinced the following morning when I told him that the game was on like Donkey

Kong at West High. I caught him in the kitchen, glumly eating cereal while listening with fading hope to radio reports on school closures in an effort to prove me wrong.

Which bugged me. A lot, actually. Why can't my kids just take my word for stuff? So then I started with him. "Well guess what," I told my glum cereal-eating son, "I never even HEARD of a snow day when I was growing up. And let me tell you, there was snow when I was growing up. Lots of snow. Big Snow. Everywhere you looked. Snow, snow, snow. We had snow coming out of ears when I was growing up. Ear snow. That's what we had. Lots of Ear Snow. Everywhere you looked. Miles and miles of Ear Snow."

I wasn't finished. Not even close.

"When your dad and I were kids in Provo, we got up at 4:00 in the morning just to milk the family cows. And when we were done with our cows, we went looking for other people's cows. We stood on street corners and shouted, come here all you other people's cows so we can milk you. EVEN THOUGH IT'S 4:00 IN THE MORNING AND THE STREETS ARE COVERED WITH EAR SNOW!"

Now here's the thing. While I was in the middle of this rant, I kind of believed what I was saying—i. e. that as a young girl growing up in Utah County, I leapt out of bed at the wintry crack of dawn to help my family out on the cow front.

But of course my family didn't have actual cows. Just a dog. And I never ever got out of bed at 4:00. Unless it was 4:00 in the afternoon.

We had snow, though. I wasn't lying about that part.

Anyhoo! My son just stared at me. I could tell by the look on his face that he was thinking oh no! My mom has Crazy Old People's Disease! Pretty soon she'll be wandering around town with her wig on backwards and her teeth in her purse, because that's where this is definitely headed.

So my boy put his spoon down. Slowly. And backed out of the room. Also slowly. Then he grabbed his coat and his backpack and RAN all the way to school where he discovered that hahahahha I was right. It wasn't a snow day after all.

Yes! Score one for the mom.

OO LA LA! THE FRENCH PROFESSOR AND MOI!

First Published March 2012

This is a story about me telling the truth.
Mostly.

A friend recently expressed concern that her oldest child will soon have a driver's license, and I went, "Oh, don't worry! She'll be fine! You'll be fine!"

Meanwhile, I secretly remembered the day I ran into a French professor's VW shortly after getting my own license.

In retrospect one of my favorite details is that the French professor, a thoroughly awesome man who lived in our neighborhood, drove a VW in the first place, even though he had six kids and a small dog that bit people. You could do that in those reckless days before Americans believed in seat belts. Everybody sat on everybody's lap and got to know each other real well—especially on long trips—and nobody gave the arrangement a second thought.

My family had a VW, too, and it was (in fact) the car I

was driving when I ran into the French professor. I know! Awesome image! Two VWs colliding!

Anyway, I was hauling downhill like my hair was on fire because I was late. And back in the day when I was late (and my hair was on fire), you did NOT want to get in my way, even if I was the one with the YIELD sign and you weren't.

Apparently, however, no one sent out that memo to the population at large. So as I was hauling and planning to hang a quick right turn, the French professor suddenly appeared in the intersection just ahead with a car crammed full of people.

Seriously, it was like a clown car. I'm pretty sure all of the French professor's kids were in there, along with the biting dog, as well as a few neighbors and also some visiting dignitaries from France such as the French president and the French president's wife and also the French president's French mistress. So you get the picture. The car was REALLY full, and it didn't stop because it had the right of way. And I didn't stop because (I don't know) I kind of forgot to.

I'll never forget the look on everybody's faces as I hurtled like a meteor toward them. Their eyes went wide and their mouths turned into little "o's", and it was clear that the French president was yelling "Mon Dieu! Mon Dieu!" as his wife and his mistress took the opportunity to start pulling each other's hair out.

Meanwhile, the French professor was all, "I can't believe that this is going to happen. But I'm pretty sure it is."

And it did.

Fortunately, the thing turned out to be a fender bender. No one was hurt. And the French professor, who graciously took care of the repairs himself, never reminded me of our chance encounter again.

So see? I mostly told the truth when I assured the concerned mother that her daughter would be okay. I just

133

didn't mention that there will be "incidents" along the way. Oh yes. There will be "incidents."

There are always incidents on the Road to Fine. But what's the point of mentioning that fact?

We all find out for ourselves sooner or later.

This is my brother, Jimmy (Judy). I used to make him wear a plastic wig to get the mail so that people would think I had a little sister. Later, my mom gave him home perms. As an adult, he is happy to be lord and master of his own hair.

We left the rest of Quinton at home.

OUT AND ABOUT

My dad traveled (a lot!) for work, and whenever possible he took us with him. Then, when I grew up, I married a man who has a fondness for the open road. This means I've had a chance to get out and about. WHICH IS AWESOME. Somehow my senses sharpen whenever I leave home and I see things, once again, with a young person's eyes.

Not my young eyes, though. I've worn glasses since the fourth grade.

Included in this section are a few pieces I wrote after traveling there and back.

Boys at the beach.

Boys at Bryce Canyon.

KNITTING ON THE BEACH

First Published July 2011

Today I want to talk about "Parental Hobbies that Might Possibly Embarrass Your Children." But first I want to tell you about "The Lady Who Turned Knitting into an Extreme Sport."

So, okay. I didn't know her personally, but everyone where I grew up knew who she was. Like the woman with the tortoise shell comb who used to sell cosmetics at Auerbach's, The Lady Who Turned Knitting was iconic. For one thing she had real presence, born of a can-do, straight-shooting attitude. She'd walk into any room and boom! You knew she was there.

Also, there was the knitting thing.

Wherever she went, this woman took her knitting along for the ride. I once saw her at a luncheon sitting at a table, knitting away while everyone around her tucked into the cheesecake.

Where I saw her most often, however, was at basketball games, decked out in colors from head to toe. Dude. The

Lady Who Turned Knitting knew how to represent.

And holy cow could she ever work magic with yarn and a pair of needles! While players stormed up and down the court like runaway freight trains, her fingers flat-out flew. I'm guessing if she were on her A-game, The Lady Who Turned Knitting could produce four afghans per game in front of the home crowd—five if things went into overtime.

A life-long knitter myself, I was in complete awe of her ability. Also her attitude! Who cared if knitting in front of 23,000 spectators looked mildly eccentric? She was all, "Yo. I do what I want." Me, I could never knit in public like that.

Or so I thought....

Lately, I have started to knit in public. Why? The older I get, the more ADD I feel. Sitting for any length of time—especially in meetings—is physically painful. But here's what I've discovered: knitting helps me to NOT fly out of my seat, run around the room, and bang my head against all four walls. Plus, check out this bonus. I've also discovered that knitting in public makes your kids squirm. WHICH IS AWESOME!

They're all, " Really, Mom? We're eating hamburgers at Hires and you're knitting socks again?"

And I'm all, "Watch me, suckers!"

Then I throw down a "sl st, k1, PSSO, k1" combination, after which I shout "boo-yah," as well as "who's your daddy!"

Embarrassing your kids in public is good for them, right? It totally builds character! And, in fact, the more embarrassed my kids are, the bolder I get. That's why I've been sitting on the beach this week with them down here in Southern California, knitting a pink baby blanket. In broad daylight! And life has been great! Until I started looking at myself through the eyes of the family renting the beach house next to ours.

So okay. About this family. There's a lot of tan-ness going on with these people. Also lots of chest muscles. Also lots of fist-pumping. If they were a reality TV show, this tan, chestally-endowed family would be Jersey Shore.

Meanwhile, they're looking at me with my Utah license plate, knitting a pink baby blanket on the beach, and going "Yep. Sister Wives."

And this, it must be said, has achieved the result my kids have only dreamed of. As we speak, I'm putting down my needles (slowly), raising my hands in the air (slowly), and backing away (also slowly) from that baby blanket.

Because you know how it is. Some things can just wait until we get back to Hires.

A COUPLE OF THINGS I LEARNED WHILE BIKING ACROSS HOLLAND

First Published July 2016

    Four summers ago, some girlfriends and I walked from coast to coast along Hadrian's Wall in Northern England. Along the way we encountered rain, mud, fields of stinging nettle, murderous sheep, an innkeeper with a mail order bride who tried to double-charge us, rain, grown men dressed like Roman soldiers, teenage boys dressed like Roman soldiers, rain, Americans who wondered why there are no washcloths in England, a lady in the middle of nowhere with a pug named Wesley selling cups of tea to hikers (the lady, not the pug named Wesley), dog enthusiasts who spent the night running their Labrador retrievers up and down the hallway outside our room, rain and cows.

    Also more rain. Also more cows.

    Good times! Which is why four years later we got together again for another adventure. This time we rode bicycles through the Netherlands and Belgium. Among other things, I'm happy to report, I learned how to ride up an escalator with a bike. (HINT: you get OFF the bike.)

Anyway, I'm back now. But the experience has caused me to reflect on the differences in the biking cultures a) here in Salt Lake City and b) there in the Low Countries. For what it's worth, here are some observations.

1. **Everybody bikes in the Netherlands and Belgium.** And by "everybody," I mean EVERYBODY. Women. Men. Girls. Boys. Babies. Pugs named Wesley. Everybody bikes—a reality that has less to do with being all progressive and "green" than it does with the fact that folks over there have been biking, biking, biking since the Middle Ages.

Biking as a primary mode of transportation hasn't caught on in Salt Lake yet, in spite of the former mayor's efforts to make our city bicycle-friendly. Americans in general and Westerners in particular are in love with cars. Dude. We practically invented cars in this country. Or at least we figured out how to mass-produce them so that ordinary people could afford them. Asking us to trade in our cars (especially the ones with cup holders) for bikes is just asking too, too much.

2. **Also! Hills!**

Here's the thing about the Netherlands. It's flat. How flat is it? Flatter than an open can of Dr Pepper left on the kitchen counter overnight. SERIOUSLY SO FLAT. Belgium is slightly hillier, but only just. This means you can bike across both countries and back in about 10 minutes without breaking a sweat—that is, if you don't stop for lunch.

Biking in Salt Lake City, on the other hand, can feel like a mountain climb in the Tour de France minus all that spandex.

3. **And here's another thing. Cars in the Netherlands and Belgium don't try to kill you.**

When I returned my mom asked if riding a bike on city streets had made me nervous. Much to my great surprise it hadn't. Why? Because I never had the sense that people were mad at me for sharing the road.

I'm often annoyed with cyclists here in Salt Lake. Too often local cyclists behave like both cars AND pedestrians—depending on the situation. Because they don't always follow the rules of the road, it's hard to predict what they're gonna do. Which makes me nervous. Which then makes me (OKAY, I ADMIT IT) feel hostile. Which makes the cyclists hostile in return.

Hey, Cyclists and Cars! Let's all give each other a little love, okay?

4. **Finally, no one wears helmets.** Except for the Americans. And possibly a few Canadians. Clearly Officer Friendly has NOT been visiting schools in Amsterdam, informing children (and their parents) about the importance of wearing protective headgear. Yo, Officer Friendly! What's up with that?

When in Rome, however . . .

Toward the end of the week I actually took off my helmet and packed it away. I'm pretty sure I didn't look Dutch or Belgian—or Roman—peddling through the countryside with my bare head.

But wow. I sure did feel like a kid again.

FIVE THINGS I RECENTLY LEARNED ON A TRIP TO THE LONE STAR STATE

First Published February 2015

Y'all!

I just got back from Texas where I spent some time with my Texas kin. And as always whenever I visit them, I learned a few new things about America's big old Lone Star. So file this one under "Stuff You Might Possibly Want to Know About Texas in Case You Ever Visit My Kin in Texas."

(And yes. It's another list. Because clearly I'm in a list-making mode these days.)

1. A GARAGE IS A GARAGE IS A GARAGE—EXCEPT WHEN IT'S A MAN CAVE.

Here's the deal. In all the years that we've been married, my husband and I have never had a garage to call our own. We park on the street. Me, I don't care. A garage is just another room to clean. But my husband wants a garage the way that a Brazilian beauty queen wants to snatch a crown off another Brazilian beauty queen's head.

"Why do you want a garage so much?" I ask him.

He looks at me like I'm nuts. Then he draws me a really big picture and answers in a loud, slow voice. "So. We. Can. Park. A. Car. In. It."

I've assumed this was a universal guy desire—until I went to Texas and walked around on a Sunday night where I discovered that absolutely no one in my kids' neighborhood uses their garages for cars. Instead these guys use them for rugs and big screen TVs and fridges full of beer and space heaters and grills and smokers and signs on the wall, including the Texas flag.

2. SPEAKING OF WHICH—THE TEXAS FLAG LOOKS A LOT LIKE THE NATIONAL FLAG OF CHILE. I'm serious. They both have a big white stripe. They both have a big red stripe. They both have a field of navy blue with a single king-sized star in the middle of it.

3. BUT WHATEVER. WHO REALLY CARES ABOUT FLAGS? Especially when you can have a PROM PICTURE taken with an alligator when you're in Texas! Do you see that photo of me there? Looking nervous? That's because my special prom date is just a few feet behind me and he looks NOTHING AT ALL like his come-on-and-date-me photos online. My Texas prom date has scaly skin. And protruding eyeballs on the side of his head. And a serious overbite. Ew! Someone call a dentist! Also, I don't see a corsage there, so he obviously forgot to buy me one. Dude! Where's my corsage? GIRL WANTS A CORSAGE! Who lined me up with this loser anyway?

4. AND THEN THERE'S THAT SKY. When one of our sons was attending Utah State, his professor (who was originally from Brooklyn) interrupted a lecture to say, "I can tell you guys are all from here because you don't fall to

your knees and shout 'we're not worthy!' whenever you step outside and see Utah's awesome mountains." (AUTHOR'S NOTE: for a different version of this story, please refer to the essay "Loving the Place Where You've Always Been." Thank you!)

And it's true. I go for days without particularly noticing our mountains, but whenever I leave home I ache in my bones for them. Still. I have to say that a Texas sky has its own kind of beauty. You know how some people have faces that show every single emotion? And you may even see all of those emotions in the space of five minutes? That's what a Texas sky looks like. Big and open and changeable. Texas sky = awesome.

5. PLUS THERE'S BBQ! Oh, Texas. Thank you for your brisket and your smoked turkey, your sausage and your ribs, your sissy sauce and your not-so-sissy sauce, your slaw and your slices of soft white bread, your baked beans and your potato salad.

And thank you, Texas, for being a home away from home for my kids.

THIRTY THINGS I LEARNED WHILE WALKING ACROSS ENGLAND

First Published July 2012

    The English woman with the tight blond perm yanked her terrier's leash and looked at us like we were dead crazy when she found out we were walking the length of Hadrian's Wall. She took a deep drag on her cigarette, exhaled, and grumbled, "Well, it's the coldest, wettest summer here in 260 years, yeah."

    It was raining there in Newcastle-on-Tyne when she said this. But our little party—Doni Perkins, Caitlin Bahr, Cynthia Knoebel and I—pressed on. After all, we'd traveled to northern England to walk from coast to coast, and walk we did—on pavement, through fields and pastures, over craggy peaks and across windy moors and marshes. Along the way I learned a few things.

1. People from England and the United States do NOT speak the same language.
2. This is doubly true of people from Scotland and the United States.
3. The Scottish have a reputation for being "dour." I never saw evidence of this. The Scots we met were friendly and full of fun.
4. Especially that middle-aged member of a punk rock band who wore a kilt and sported a massive Mohawk. He and his wife checked up on their kids back home by stalking them on Facebook.
5. The claims of terrible British food are greatly exaggerated. Brits, in fact, excel at comfort food—steak and ale pie, fish and chips, fabulous curries. Also, their cheeses and tea treats—scones, shortbread, cakes—are to die for.
6. Speaking of which, the Cadbury chocolate in England tastes better than the Cadbury chocolate here.
7. You either love bagpipe music or you don't. I triple love it.
8. Bending your left knee when you pose for a photo doesn't make you look slimmer. It just makes you look like you're bending your left knee.
9. If you ask for a "napkin" in a British restaurant in 2012, the server will bring you a napkin. This didn't used to be the case.
10. It is easier to slog through a wet sheep pasture than a wet cow pasture. WHO KNEW?!
11. It's always a little troubling when you smell something bad and realize that after spending six days walking through pastures, it's probably you.
12. Which reminds me—it's not the miles alone that make a long walk challenging. It's the condition of those miles.
13. So here's the deal: sometimes the reality of an experience doesn't coincide with your expectations.

14. Do yourself a favor and adapt quickly to your new reality, especially one involving rain.

15. Stinging nettle is aptly named. Hello! It stings! But the people at Hadrian's Hotel were right—rubbing the affected area (i.e. my right calf) with a dark green tree leaf relieves the pain. I know! Voodoo!

16. The ritual known as "afternoon tea" restores both body and soul.

17. There are tourists who walk Hadrian's Wall in togas. Everywhere I looked on this trip, I saw guys in skirts.

18. If you travel to the U.K. these days, more than one citizen will tell you that "England has changed . . . and not for the better."

19. There are undoubtedly people in northern England and Scotland who are excited about the upcoming Olympic games. But we sure didn't meet any.

20. Seriously, there is nothing prettier than a country cottage garden in full bloom.

21. What with cows mooing "here" and sheep baa-ing "there," the countryside isn't all that quiet.

22. Speaking of which—DON'T LAUGH—but sheep can feel surprisingly menacing when you're standing in the thick of them on a windy moor and there are literally no other human beings around for miles and miles.

23. You need an advanced degree in engineering to figure out how to turn on a British shower.

24. Also, we only saw one washcloth on our trip. Can somebody from the U.K. please tell us where all the damn washcloths went?

25. Pleasant walking companions—those you see every day, as well as the ones you meet along the way—are a joy to be with.

26. If you want to do the Wall Walk for yourself, I'd advise

you to travel from east to west. The Romans built the wall that way, and as our guidebook says, the scenery improves when you head in that direction.
27. Have faith in the journey you've chosen.
28. However, you might not want to take that journey during the rainiest summer in 260 years.
29. Still, I would not have missed the experience for the world. The endless vistas of field, stone and sky will be with me always.
30. Which reminds me—it's easy to look at your feet the entire time you walk across England. Remember to look up.
You'll be glad you did.

DEAR NATIONAL PARK SERVICE

First Published June 2016

Dear National Parks Service,

HAPPY BIRTHDAY! You're 100 years old now and to celebrate, my husband and I spent last weekend in and around Capitol Reef. OK. Kidding. We weren't there for your birthday. We just wanted to go. But still. HAPPY BIRTHDAY!

Personally, I'm glad you're around, and here's something we discovered on this recent trip: it's even more fun to visit a national park without the kids! I didn't have to tell my husband to stop crying. I also didn't have to promise I'd buy him a Slurpee as soon as we finished hiking. Not even once. Score! See? There are some advantages to being aging Baby Boomers.

But that's not the point.

The point is that because of you there are wild places left to visit. And of all the wild places left to visit, Capitol Reef and the surrounding areas are probably my favorite. Why?

Well, you've got that color thing going on there. Everywhere you look there are rocks the color of blood and elephants, salt and lilacs, cocoa and moss, fool's gold and raspberries, topped with silvery plants and dead trees rising up against a cerulean sky like black antlers.

I like the sounds there, too. As I drifted off to sleep the first night, I thought I heard the familiar rush of downtown traffic—a sound I routinely hear on summer evenings through my open window. But then I realized it was the wind, playing through the trees. I heard crickets, as well, and birds during the day, including the raspy croak of a raven.

Here's another park pleasure—looking for shapes in stones. Some of the formations look like people—Christmas carolers huddling together on a front porch, a row of stout great-aunts looking down on visitors and passing judgment, a boxer with bare knuckles showing, the faces on Mt. Rushmore only partially carved.

Other formations look like objects—toy transformers, a bike helmet, mushrooms, a row of garbage cans upended by a windstorm, sheets of ribbon cake, a mask discarded by the Phantom of the Opera, skulls bleached clean by relentless light, a crouching gnome, those monoliths on Easter Island.

Still other formations recall structures, especially places of worship—cathedrals and synagogues, temples and mosques with minarets. There are skyscrapers, too. Hello, Fifth Avenue! You want some Roman ruins and medieval fortresses? Capitol Reef is your place.

Oh. And don't forget the rocks that look like animals—a colony of Emperor Penguins, a chimp on a ledge surveying the stone jungle below, a half-submerged hippo, the heads of a turtle and a buffalo, a sea lion sunning.

So yeah. The park is a feast for the senses. But what I

love the best—the very best—is that feeling I experience of hurtling back through space and time to stand in an ancient place where life has gone on for years and years and will go on for years and years after I leave this earth. A place where junipers reveal blue-green berries like jewels season after season. A place where wind and water take a thousand years to shape a single stone. A place that always invites you to remember that the world is so much larger than you yourself and the burdens you carry.

    A place that invites you to put those burdens aside—at least for now—while you stop and listen to the sound of a breeze and your own heart beating.

Sincerely,
Ann Cannon

COWS, ALIENS AND ALL THAT JAZZ

First Published February 2011

    Today I'm going to talk about something I learned this week.
    But first I want to tell you about my trip out to Dugway this past Wednesday.
    I know! Dugway! How often do ordinary civilians like me get the chance to visit the base out there? So when I was invited to give a presentation for the Utah Humanities Council at the post library, I saluted and said yes sir! (Snappily.)
    I was excited to visit Dugway for a number of reasons. When our family moved from Utah to New York state, I assumed I'd miss the view of mountains to the east. As it turned out what I REALLY missed was the view of desert to the west. Hemmed in by thick towering trees everywhere I looked in New York, I yearned for wide open spaces. I yearned for an ocean of sage and a sea of sky meeting at the shoreline of some distant horizon.

So, yeah. I do like the desert. And I looked forward to driving through Skull Valley in the wheat-colored light of late afternoon. Besides, I could get a column out of the experience, right? I could write about the ghost town Iosepa—that unlikely and ill-fated Polynesian settlement north of DPG. It would be a melancholy column to match my wintry melancholy mood. Something about the death of dreams and so forth.

But while I was driving I got all distracted by cows. Who knew there were so many cows in Skull Valley? Cows to the left of me! Cows to the right! There I was, stuck in the middle with cows!

So then I started thinking about cows and how it might be fun to own one. It's true they're kinda stupid. But then I don't necessarily value intelligence in an animal above all else, unlike certain border collie owners who are always happy to point out their dog is on the honor roll while your kid is not. Besides, what evidence do they have that their border collie is smarter than your kid? That their dog can jump into the air and catch a Frisbee with its mouth? Please.

But whatever. The point is I thought a cow might be fun to own because you know how cows are—sweet and gentle and full of potential ice cream.

At any rate, I arrived at Dugway, did my presentation, and met some very nice people in the process. In fact, these people were so nice they warned me to be careful on my drive home.

Okay. When they first started to warn me, I thought they were going to say, "Watch out for aliens." In fact, that's what I hoped they were going to say because hey! I could totally get a good column out of that! But instead they said, "Watch out for cows."

Seriously? They wanted me to watch out for cows?

Didn't they know that cows are our friends?

Except not so much in the dead of night, as it turns out. My new Dugway friends were right. Those same black angus cows that seem so happy and cheerful by the light of day suddenly feel sinister and menacing standing darkly on the side of the road. You feel like an interloper stumbling onto gang turf and that at any minute those cows are gonna jump you in the middle of the street, just like the Jets and the Sharks. Only in this case, they would be the Cow Jets and the Cow Sharks. And also they wouldn't be wearing tight pants.

Anyway. Back to the beginning. What did I learn this week? I could say I learned that things don't always turn out the way you think they will. Like, for instance, you think you're going to miss the mountains but instead you miss the desert. Or you think you might write a touching column about Iosepa and instead you write about livestock. A lot of life is like that, actually. Surprising.

But here's what I actually learned, you guys: cows can be scary.

Party hats

CELEBRATION TIME (COME ON!)

I like holidays.

No.

I LOVE holidays. I love to decorate for holidays. I love to write about holidays.

I take after my great-grandmother Pat this way, who knew how to party on whenever a holiday rolled around. Also, she slept with a shotgun. But that's another story.

In this section, you'll find columns about (wait for it) holidays!

Nothing says "Happy Easter" like breaking eggs over your head.

Christmas long, long ago. The woman with the white hair is my pistol-packing great-grandmother, Patti Larsen.

RESOLUTIONS

First Published January 2012

    I don't always make New Year's Resolutions. And when I do, I don't always make them for myself.

    Sometimes I make them for family members. ("We, Ann Cannon's married kids, promise to move back to Utah with her grandchildren after we finish graduate school.")

    Sometimes I make them for famous people. ("We, the Kardashians, promise to turn into nuns and take vows of silence until the end of time.")

    Sometimes I make them for my dogs. ("Me, Zora, promise not to stick big furry head in toilet bowl during year of 2012.")

    Here's what I have discovered, however: making resolutions for other people (also dogs!) is generally about as successful as making them for myself.

    Still! Hope springs eternal, which is why last Saturday I made up a list of resolutions . . . and okay FINE. You're right. I've already tossed most of them into the recycling bin, where they will (no doubt) be waiting for me when next year rolls around.

She shoots! She scores!

At least I haven't abandoned this resolution: to send more hand-written notes.

My co-worker Rachel gave me the idea. Facing the holidays with a minimum of cash for gifts, Rachel decided to write her friends personal little letters, detailing the qualities she admires in them. She slipped me a note right before Christmas, and it seriously ended up being one of my favorite presents.

I loved everything about it—the sentiments, of course, but also the pretty paper it was written on, as well as the look of Rachel's handwriting, which is so much like Rachel herself—exuberant and feminine.

Another friend, Stephanie, also sent me a hand-written letter over the holidays. It was chatty, newsy—full of sharp observations about people and events.

Reading these letters from Rachel and Stephanie caused me to reflect on how impersonal so much of our written communication has become. One email looks very much like another email. Same with texts. If the sender's name weren't attached, would you even know who sent it to you?

But a handwritten letter is different. A person's handwriting is as unique as thumbprints. It's individual. Quirky. Revealing. I look at a piece of scrap paper with a telephone number scrawled across it and recognize immediately which son wrote it. Their handwriting is part of their identity.

Not long ago I came across a note sent to me by my friend Marilyn shortly before she died of colon cancer. Of course I have vivid memories of Marilyn—the sound of her laugh, the way she cocked her head to the side when you told her a story, the scent of her perfume. She was one of those people who took the party with her wherever she went, and so far she's proven to be pretty unforgettable.

Still. I'm grateful for the piece of paper signed, "Xoxox, Marilyn." It's a tangible reminder of the huge presence she was in my life for so many years.

So here's to 2012 . . . and to a mailbox full of notes.

HEARTS ON FIRE

First Published February 2017

Dear Elementary School Kids,
    Don't look now but Valentine's Day is right around the corner!
    Oh. Wait. You've looked already? And you're busy trying to figure out if that special girl or boy in your class has noticed you? It's kinda hard to tell, right? Because (no offense, Kids) you're not very good at communicating "romantic interest" to one another.
    That's why I asked friends to share the things they did to attract attention when they were your age. Hopefully their experiences will help you understand what's really going on when that boy sitting across the cafeteria table from you suddenly picks up his lunch fork and starts combing his hair with it.
    That's what my son did in the second grade btw. He wanted to impress the cute girl sitting across the table from him, so he—you know—groomed. (P.S. It didn't work.)
    Anyway. If you notice classmates engaging in any of the

following behaviors around you—no matter how weird—they're probably trying to get your attention.

Talking in a scary voice: My friend Kerry related that when the boy she liked gave their teacher some flowers, she stopped him in his tracks and said in a scary voice: "I know you brought one of those for me, right?"

Looking away whenever you show up: Shy kids don't know what to do with their feelings. So they turn their faces whenever you walk into their line of vision. But rest assured they're giving you some serious side eye.

Making "rating calls": Kids are bolder when they're in a group, which is why they call you when they get together and ask you to rate them on a scale of 1-10. Or at least kids did this when everybody had landlines. They probably aren't calling your parents' cellphones and asking them to rate you.

Sending Love Notes: Some kids are better at writing down their feelings than speaking them. My friend Venna remembers the note she received from a boy in her class: "Roses are red, violets are blue, you have a nose, like a B-52."

Giving Chase: Okay, Kids. If someone is chasing you around the playground like a maniac at recess, you can be pretty sure he or she is interested

Kissing you behind the dumpster at recess: See above.

Throwing spit wads: I used to throw spit wads on the bus at boys I liked, because you know how it is—nothing says "Dude! I love you!" like a spit wad launched from the back of the bus.

Using Nicknames: Actually, this one's tricky. Sometimes kids WANT you to feel bad when they call you a name. One of the older boys in our neighborhood, for example, used to call me "Machinegun Annie" because he said I sounded like a machine gun whenever I laughed. RUDE! My friend Marti remembers classmates calling her "Farty Marti" and her first-grade boyfriend "Smelly Kelly" just to be mean. Fortunately, Farty Marti and Smelly Kelly had each other, so everything worked out in the end.

Putting extra candy in your valentine envelope: Extra candy is a sure sign that someone is crushing on you. Also, if you're a boy, pay attention to the sentiments on the conversation hearts you get from a girl. Chances are good that she spent hours choosing them just for you. If you're a girl, however, don't bother to decode. Like my friend Cynthia says, the boy's mom probably stuffed the envelopes for him the night before the class party.

I hope this helps, Kids. Just remember that romance is easier when you're an adult.

Not.

Sincerely,
Ann Cannon

WHAT TO DO ON A SATURDAY WHEN YOU'RE AN EMPTY NESTER IN 25 EASY STEPS

First Published April 2017

1. Yay! It's Saturday! And now that all your kids have grown up and moved out, you're totally free to do whatever you want to!
2. This wasn't true back in the day. You spent Saturday mornings going to soccer games and baseball games and football games. Also, you went to the grocery store on Saturday mornings when you suddenly went YIKES! IT'S MY TURN TO BRING THE TREATS!
3. So then you raced to the store and bought healthy crap like oranges so the other parents wouldn't judge you for bringing unhealthy crap like Twinkies. Which is what YOU'D choose to eat instead of stupid oranges if you

were a kid. But you buy fruit. Buying Fruit = Responsible Parenting.

4. Now that your own kids are gone, you watch your neighbors load their kids in the car and feel happy that those days are in your rearview mirror.

5. Mostly. The truth is you sometimes feel nostalgic for those days.

6. Also, what are you going to do with yourself on a Saturday? You could clean the house but blech. Where's the fun in that?

7. Then you remember that when you were at PetSmart last week, a guy handed you a flier saying that the Easter Bunny would be there on Saturday so you could have your dog take a picture with him.

8. Wait, I said to the guy. The Easter Bunny?

9. Yeah, said the guy. It'll be me in an Easter Bunny suit.

10. Was that part in the job description? I asked. You dressing up like a big rabbit?

11. It'll be fun! He said. You and your dog should come!

12. It's Saturday now, so I say to my husband, how about we take our Newfoundland named Tinkerbell to get her picture taken with the Easter Bunny today? My husband doesn't even act like this sounds weird. He just says okay. Why not?

13. So we put Tinkerbell in the car and drive to PetSmart so she can have her picture taken with the Easter Bunny.

14. We don't tell her that it's not the real Easter Bunny. What she doesn't know won't hurt her.

15. When we get there we see other people who want their dogs to have pictures taken with the Easter Bunny, too.

16. The lady in front of us has two little dogs dressed in shirts. The Easter Bunny sits them on his Easter Bunny lap and makes those little dogs wave their paws at us. Wave! Wave! Wave!

17. Their legs aren't very long, so those little dogs look like they're waving at us with tiny T-Rex arms. Wave! Wave! Wave!

18. And now it's our turn. Yay!

19. Except Tinkerbell is suddenly wondering what the hell we are doing here with a fake rabbit the size of a human being. She starts acting like a calf in a calf-roping contest. GET ME OUT OF HERE!

20. Luckily, I have excellent calf roping skills. Soon, Tinkerbell and I are ready to pose for the camera.

21. Do you mind if I sit on your lap, I ask the Easter Bunny. I think the picture will look better if we all get cozy.

22. The Easter Bunny doesn't say anything.

23. Maybe he doesn't say anything because he wants to stay in character. Or possibly he thinks I'm hitting on him.

24. Dude oughta realize I'm married. And even if I weren't, I've always made it a point not to date large rabbits.

25. Finally our picture gets taken! Just in time for me and mine to wish you and yours a fine Easter weekend.

FATHERS

First Published June 2012

Over the years people have had interesting reactions upon discovering we have five sons. When we lived in New York, for example, folks would gasp in astonishment and say, "God Bless!"—except for one man who looked at our Utah license plate and (true story) asked, "So what are you guys? A singing group?"

The most common reaction I've had, however, is this: "Five boys? Well! Five boys would be a LOT easier than five girls, because girls are so emotional."

Okay. I do know something about emotional girls because I was one. I remember the time my dad took me golfing on a muggy Illinois day when I was 14. I was wearing hot pants (striped) and a new pair of sandals, and I kept flipping my bangs out of my eyes like I was Farrah Fawcett. After the first hole I started to complain because my clubs were so HEAVY and ew (!) there were bugs EVERYWHERE and also it was so HUMID and everybody was ew (!) SWEATING, which was completely GROSS, and also my sandals were giving me BLISTERS, and why did we have to play stupid boring golf anyway when we could have gone to a movie instead where there was air conditioning and tubs of buttered popcorn and possibly BOYS who were not my ew (!) brothers?

My dad didn't say anything to stem the tsunami of whining that flowed freely from my mouth. He just kept swinging his golf club with that air of quiet desperation stoic men display on death marches. But I did catch him looking at me once or twice like he wished 14-year-old daughters had never been invented.

So yeah. I get it. Girls can be emotional.

Still. I'm surprised when people assume that boys aren't—that somehow they're these easy-going creatures who take acne, girl trouble, difficult coaches, troublesome math classes, hormones, body image issues, and parental expectations all in stride.

And maybe there are boys like that somewhere—boys who are just all "hakuna matata." But those boys didn't live at our house.

One of our sons, in particular, had a (instead of "stormy," let's put "REALLY emotional") adolescence. In sheer frustration, he once punched a hole in the upstairs wall. Yowza! And there the hole stayed until that son went away to college, mostly because we never got around to fixing it. We didn't intend for the hole to be a gaping reminder of a bad family moment. But still. There it was.

Fast forward to the week before our son came home. I found my husband in the hallway late one night, patching up that hole at long last. Watching him, I realized that more than an act of delayed maintenance, filling in that hole with joint compound was an act of love. It was a father's way of saying the past is behind us. Let bygones be bygones.

Welcome home.

Talk about emotion!

I am grateful to my husband for that and all the other gestures he makes to be a good parent. Happy Father's Day to him and all you dads out there who try to do right by your sons and your daughters.

AND SUDDENLY IT'S THE FOURTH OF JULY

First Published July 2013

    I always compare the progression of a year to a train ride. The first half of the year, that train is chugging uphill like the little engine that could, huffing and puffing and saying, "I think I can! I think I can!"

    Then July hits.

    And suddenly you're careening down the backside of the year in a runaway freight train, barreling toward December at breakneck speed, shouting at mountain goats to. Just. Get. Out. Of. The. Way.

    At least that's how it feels to me. Which is why as soon as the Fourth of July is over, I always say you oughta just put up your Christmas tree and be done with it, because the holidays will be here before we all know it.

    When I was a kid Christmas was far and away my favorite holiday. What's not to love about a celebration where a stranger dressed in brushed velveteen breaks into your house in the middle of the night and puts stuff in your socks?

I liked the Fourth of July, too. What's not to love about a holiday where all the teenage boys in your neighborhood try to blow things up? It's just that if I were the Bachelorette when I was a kid, and I had to choose between Christmas (a.k.a. "Brooks," the hometown guy) and the Fourth of July (a.k.a "Juan Pablo" who is "muy caliente" according to my nieces), I would have definitely given Christmas the rose and asked him to stick around for awhile.

It's not that I don't like Christmas now. I do. I love the lights and the colors, the music and the scents. It's just that when you grow up, you realize that Christmas is a LOT of work. Especially for the moms. That's when you start to appreciate holidays that are a little more laid back. Like Arbor Day, for example.

And yes. The Fourth of July, too.

The Fourth is great because there's lots to do that moms aren't in charge of—a Bees baseball game, the city parade, the Stadium of Fire.

You're also not expected to decorate very much. We hang some bunting on the front porch, stick a few flags and red-white-and-blue windmill toys in the flowerpots and call it good. In fact, we don't call that good. We call that awesome. And also patriotic!

Even if you're in charge of a picnic, you can just show up with a bucket of KFC and no one will call you a slacker, which is exactly what your family and friends WOULD call you if you served the same thing on Christmas Day. Am I right?

Or you can do what our family does—make food assignments, which means (among other things) that you will be treated to my mother-in-law's famous potato salad.

After all these years, I'm still not sure why her potato

salad is so outstanding. It's pretty straightforward, actually. Potatoes are involved, of course. Some Mayo. A little mustard. Onion salt. A tiny bit of sweet relish juice. And yet it makes all other potato salads ashamed to call themselves potato salads.

Meanwhile, everyone pulls up a chair to eat, to watch kids run through the sprinklers, to enjoy the feel of summer on the skin, to acknowledge that in spite of her faults this is, in fact, a great country.

Have a Happy Fourth!

(And then go get yourselves a tree, already.)

WHO DOESN'T LOVE A DOG IN COSTUME?

First Published October 2011

    I've never bothered to dress up our dogs for Halloween. Lining up costumes for the kids was challenging enough back in the day. Fortunately I had a bunch of boys who were completely low-maintenance on the wardrobe front. They were happy to be "Pizza Delivery Guys" for Halloween. You hand a kid an empty Little Caesar's pizza box along with a hairnet and voila! Instant costume!

    Last year, however, I decided it would be all kinds of fun to dress up our enormous Newfoundland dog. So I rooted through the old dress-up box, found a flannel shirt and a cowboy hat and decided Zora could be the Marlboro Man for Halloween.

    So let me say right here that dressing a 200-pound dog presents certain challenges. It's sort of like dressing a cow. It's not that cows are deliberately uncooperative when you try to put clothes on them as much as they're just these enormous immovable objects. They stand there, giving you vacant looks exactly like the looks you gave your parents when you were 14 years old and your parents asked you why you were getting a D-plus in P.E. and you just stared back at them, because who cared about P.E. and what was wrong with your parents anyway? Didn't they know it was time to go meet your friend Gigi Ballif at the mall?

So yeah. Dressing Zora up was the same kind of experience. But whatever. I managed, and wow! When all was said and done, she looked pretty great in her hat with all that dog fur billowing out of her flannel shirt just like it was Marlboro Man chestal hair.

Are you getting some kind of visual here?

Pleased with the result, I told my son to take Zora on a walk around the block, just to strut her Marlboro Man stuff. Except when the two of them came back, I could tell from my son's face that something unfortunate had happened.

"What's wrong?" I asked.

"Some lady screamed at me."

"Why?"

"She said I was demeaning my dog."

Okay. Do you have a problem with strangers who self-righteously scold strangers just because someone has a dog dressed up like a cowboy? Because I do. Unless there's something really egregious happening, I think people ought to resist the impulse to lecture their fellow citizens and just leave each other alone.

"But here's the worst part, Mom," said my son. "The lady who screamed at me was packing around a Chihuahua. IN A BABY SNUGGLY."

Which is another awesome visual, right? Seriously, it's hard to resist the image of a woman with a Chihuahua strapped across her bosom yelling at a boy walking a large dog wearing a hat.

Anyway. Another Halloween has rolled around, which brings me to the point of this column. Do you, in fact, think it's demeaning to dress a dog up like Yoda? Or Elvis? Or the Flying Nun? Would you? Have you? Will you again?

Speak up.

(And while you're at it, have a Happy Halloween.)

THANKSGIVING THE FIRST

First Published November 2016

    I have no idea how they talk about the First Thanksgiving in elementary schools these days.

    When I was growing up, teachers told us that the Pilgrims and the Native Americans decided to have a party to celebrate the fact that the Native Americans taught the Pilgrims how not to die that first year. Score!

    So here's the way that first Thanksgiving went down. Everyone had an assignment. The Pilgrims brought the green bean casserole and that yam dish with those melted marshmallows on the top. The Native Americans brought the turkey and the stuffing, as well as the corn. I can't remember who brought the rolls, but the Native Americans and Pilgrims all brought pies for a friendly after-dinner competition to see who made the best desserts.

    Meanwhile, people had so much fun they decided to make Thanksgiving an annual tradition, which all Americans observe to this day.

    My own kids heard pretty much the same story when

they were in elementary school. Maybe they even remember who brought the rolls. I'll have to ask.

But "sacred narratives"—those stories that a group of people tell themselves about themselves—have a way of changing with the times. Why does this happen? Sometimes a narrative falls out of favor because it's just not true (SPOILER ALERT: George Washington did not chop down a cherry tree. His first biographer, Mason Weems, made it up to emphasize Washington's honesty. Irony! And also sorry if this fact ruins your day.)

Sometimes a traditional narrative will change because it expands to tell a more complex truth. When I was growing up, for example, Christopher Columbus was universally portrayed as a hero who discovered America—even if he got mixed up and thought "America" was actually "India." But whatever. Back in those days people were often confused about which continents they were visiting.

When people talk about Christopher Columbus now, they often mention that while his discovery was a good thing for Europeans, it was a bad thing for the indigenous people who already lived here. Which is true.

Also, he wasn't even the first white guy to show up in the Americas. Leif Erickson and his crew of Vikings (plus one German named Thyrker) beat Columbus to the punch. They came. They did Viking things. They went home and drank mead.

Also, some people now think the Chinese showed up here 70 years or so before Columbus did. That's the premise of the book *1421* by historian Gavin Menzies.

WHO KNEW AMERICA WAS SUCH A POPULAR PLACE TO DISCOVER?

But that's not the point. The point is this: sacred narratives change.

Still, I want to believe there's more than an element of truth to the traditional Thanksgiving story. I want to think that at some moment in the history of our country, people who weren't very much alike sat down together at the same table to share a few laughs and a good meal, after which everyone played a game of touch football. Even the moms.

The story of the first Thanksgiving is, in fact, one of our country's foundational stories. And it's a good story, too, even if everything went up in flames after that first friendly meal. Here's what it says about who we are as a nation—or at least who we aspire to be: a people who can accommodate one another and focus on what we have in common.

In this moment of time, it feels like we're a long way away from this ideal. Or at least it does to me. But come on. Let's keep trying.

Because why not?

FEAR NOT

First Published December 2010

It's Christmas morning, which means you're not reading this column. Instead, you're opening gifts or calling friends or attending religious services or eating an outstanding breakfast (which includes French toast I hope) or listening to Christmas music or (ah!) sleeping. And seriously I am just fine with that. I hope this day is satisfying in all the ways that matter most to you and the people you love.

Me, I'm recalling the Christmas morning I was 6 years old. That was the Christmas I spent in bed. In fact, that was the entire school year I spent in bed with acute nephritis. There was a time when that experience was never far from my thoughts. But you know how it is. Life goes on, and one day you realize you rarely think about the events, both happy and sad, that once defined you.

But here I am, suddenly remembering.

I see my father lift and carry me from my bed to the family room. I see the tree in the corner there, trimmed with gingerbread boys and shining with tinsel. I see my little brother, still in his footed pajamas, race toward his pile of presents from Santa Claus. I hear the crackle of carols on the radio as my mother enters the room with a fat baby on her hip. I hear the sound of my grandparents' voices in the kitchen. I smell cinnamon and citrus, wood smoke and pine. And when my father sets me gently down on the couch, I feel like a small happy bird resting in a nest of plump cushions and pillows.

It's a good Christmas.

That's the part I remember—how pleasant, how relaxed it all was.

And yet I know now that my parents wrestled that day with a myriad of ever present fears. Had they made the right decision to move from Salt Lake to Provo? Would my father succeed at his new job? Could they meet their mounting financial obligations, especially now that there were medical bills involved? And would their oldest child recover? Would there, in fact, be more Christmases with her at all?

Now here's the thing: it turns out that my protracted illness was a gift. Truly. Before the illness I was as restless as wind. Distractible. Impulsive. I never sat still. Ever. But those months in bed provided me with the chance to finally learn my letters and then my words, and from there I began to spin sentences and paragraphs and stories until here I am this very morning, writing a column that I hope with all my heart you're not reading because you've happily given yourself over to the morning instead.

That Christmas gave my parents and me both the chance to learn this truth—bright things often rise up from the ashes of our disasters, and that hope, if we allow it to, can trump fear.

And so this day I wish to add my voice to those long-ago voices that some say gathered high in starlit skies with this message. Fear not.

Fear not the memories of our pasts or the concerns of our presents or the uncertainty of our futures.

Fear. Not.

THROW DEEP

First Published December 2012

    I know.
    I should be writing a column about making New Year's Resolutions right now. But instead I find myself thinking about my grandma and her two sisters.
    These two sisters were photo negatives of each other. Reverse doppelgangers. The one sister was always HEY-THE-GLASS-IS-HALF-FULL-AND-IMA-GONNA-DRINK-IT-AFTER-WHICH-IMA-GONNA-DRINK-YOUR-GLASS-TOO!
    And the other sister was all, "Meh. Why should I bother to drink from a glass that's half-empty? I'd rather just die of thirst anyway. Also starvation."
    I'll never forget the time I introduced my first-born to the other sister when he was two weeks old—a mere slip of a person with just a breath of hair. I'd gone up to my mother's house where I found my great-aunt sitting in the living room in the middle of the day wearing a pink robe.
    I peeled the receiving blanket away from my baby's round

red face and presented him to my great-aunt.

She looked at him with tired eyes and pronounced, "Well, they come into this world and they go out of this world."

Then she stood up and shuffled off to Buffalo. Wearing a pink robe.

Life is so mysterious sometimes, isn't it? Why was my great-aunt sitting in my mother's living room? In the middle of the day? Wearing a pink robe?

I'm still not sure.

I was, however, sure of this: I never ever wanted to be like that great-aunt. I never wanted to be the person who could look at a brand new baby and then suck the joy straight out of a room.

Fast forward to the final days of 2012. I'm older now. There's been a lot of living since that moment I unveiled my firstborn (he's 32!), and guess what. I sort of get what that great-aunt in the pink robe was all about.

Life—even a life that is relatively free of Big Drama—has a way of wearing you down if not completely out. And, as a result, the temptation to respond with a certain amount of apathy becomes huge. Or at least it has been in my case. I feel that creeping apathy these days in the way I connect (or don't) to the things I've always enjoyed: music, books, my garden, travel, the view of mountains to the south.

Little by little I have begun to turn into a person sitting in the living room. In the middle of the day. Wearing a pink robe.

Which makes me think of a story my dad used to tell about the great NFL quarterback Kenny "the Snake" Stabler. Stabler was asked what Jack "Call of the Wild" London meant by the following quotation:

"I would rather be ashes than dust! I would rather that my spark should burn out in a brilliant blaze than it should be stifled by dry-rot. I would rather be a superb meteor, every atom of me in magnificent glow, than a sleepy and permanent planet. The function of man is to live, not to exist. I shall not waste my days trying to prolong them. I shall use my time."

Stabler replied, "Throw deep."

Maybe this story—London's statement, Stabler's response—is apocryphal. Who knows? But it speaks to me right now. So if I get around to making a New Year's resolution, it will be this: throw deep.

And if I can't throw deep, at least I'll make the effort.

One young coach

I'LL TELL YOU WHAT

Shortly after Dad died in 2016, our lovely neighbors Allen and Julie Dodworth sent me a card with this message: "Ann, keep your father in your life. Hold him tight in your heart, speak his name often, and bring him into your dreams."

I find myself keeping Dad alive by saying the things he always said. One of his favorite phrases was "I'll Tell You What." And then he'd tell you what.

I miss the sound of his voice.

This section contains columns about him that I wrote for The Salt Lake Tribune. I've also taken the liberty of adding a few additional memories of him, written during those last few months.

Dad (aka #13) wearing tiny shorts at Orem's old Lincoln High.

G.I. Dad

PRACTICALLY A MOVIE STAR

    Dad was fond of saying that a parent can parent along the way. This meant that if he had an errand to run, he'd take one of us kids with him so we could talk. This practice also extended to recruiting trips.

    Back in the day before players signed official letters of intent, coaches were tasked with the duty of making sure kids who'd committed in January to play at Brigham Young University still felt the same way a few months later. To help players honor their original commitment, Dad would stay in touch with them by paying personal visits—even if those players lived in faraway California. Which they mostly did. California was his recruiting turf when he was an assistant to Tommy Hudspeth. So when summers rolled around, Dad and Mom would toss us in the car and head west. That way Dad could be both a parent AND a coach.

    Which brings us to Barry Bic.

    That wasn't his real name. But that's the name I remember him by because he was "in the business," as Dad said. Show business. Barry Bic's family was in the business, too, and they lived in the hills overlooking L.A. Dad took us to Barry Bic's house at night, which gave me a chance to overlook the City of Angels with its hazy glittering City of Angels lights from the backyard. I was 9 years old, and it's a sight I've never forgotten.

As was Barry Bic. I've never forgotten the sight of him either.

He was lounging in the family pool (!) when my parents, my brother John and I joined him in the backyard. Barry Bic was wearing a swimming suit and suddenly I was all agog because Barry Bic looked like Sean Connery's James Bond. Or at least his chest did.

Because it was a hairy. It was really hairy. The hairiest chest alive.

This was something I'd never seen before. My own father's chest was as slick and bare-skinned as a rat's tail. And although there were probably plenty of hairy chests at the public swimming pool in Provo where I spent a lot of time during the summer, I hadn't noticed those because I was too busy pretending to be mermaids with my girlfriends.

Dad cut into my hairy-chest-induced stupor with an introduction.

"This is my daughter, Ann," he told Barry Bic. "She wants to be a movie star one day."

Okay. This was news to me. But I did like the sound of it.

From the pool where he lounged, Barry Bic smiled up at me.

"Well, if you're going to be a movie star, you gotta have a stage name," he said.

I nodded like this was yesterday's newspaper.

"So, then. What's it gonna be?" Barry Bic asked.

And in the single most impressive moment of my young life—perhaps in my entire life—I pulled a stage name straight out of the air.

"Angie Ramone," I said.

"Angie Ramone," Barry Bic repeated. He slowly nodded his approval. "I like it."

YES! BARRY BIC WHO WAS IN THE BUSINESS LIKES MY NAME!

I looked down at the glittering city below and felt like I was already one of its stars.

I LEFT MY HEART THERE TOO

First Published March 2014

Dear San Francisco,
   You were the light at the end of my tunnel.
   Let me explain.
   Once upon a time my dad played college football with a lovely and generous man who grew up to be a dentist. A dentist who eventually opened a practice in Walnut Creek, right across the bay from you. Meanwhile, my dad grew up to be a lovely and generous man with kids who had terrible teeth.
   We're talking epic terrible here.
   It's not that my brothers and I didn't take care of our teeth. We did. We brushed regularly and with real intent, and if flossing had been invented then, we would have flossed regularly and with real intent, too. Unfortunately, all that earnest brushing didn't do us much good. We still got cavities. A LOT of them. It's like all the children in our

family were born without enamel. We were the Enamel-less Ones.

At some point my parents did the math and decided that it would actually be cheaper to throw us in the station wagon, haul across the Nevada desert and visit my dad's friend who offered to do our teeth for free after hours than to have the work done at home. Thus began our yearly treks to our new family dentist.

Who lived two states away.

The dental work part wasn't fun—for us OR for the dentist. We met in his office like spies doing a live drop in the dead of night. All of us were grim-faced and anxious. How long would we be sitting in that chair—heads back and mouths open under a single naked light bulb—this time? Hours? Days? Months?

(Okay. I'm making up the part about the single naked light bulb. There were two naked light bulbs.)

And then? After hours of torture, our dentist would pronounce, "Mission Accomplished!" And all of us, including the dentist, celebrated our survival by visiting you. The City by the Bay. Like I said, you were definitely the light at the end of my tunnel.

I just loved the noise you made, San Francisco, with your gulls shrieking overhead and your streetcars roaring along on their ropes of steel and your residents serving up a full linguistic buffet. I liked the way you looked, too, with your streets and structures lined up at crazy angles and your planters full of green and growing things and your general sense of visual style. You were like Sienna Miller or Kate Moss—one of those rare women who can wear a swirling bohemian skirt with cowboy boots, a fitted blazer, a sloppy hat and somehow make it all work.

Also? Your food. It made my knees buckle. The dim

sum! The pasta! The seafood! We always took loaves of your sourdough home with us, hoarding them in the trunk of our car and hoping they would taste as good in Utah as they did on the wharf. Which they didn't. But we never stopped trying.

Oh, San Francisco. Great, glittering, gaudy San Francisco. You were the first big city I ever met, the first big city I ever had a crush on. You were my first urban love. My husband and I visited you a few weeks ago. I wondered if this time I would finally be over you. Too often the things we once loved—certain books or movies or dishes or places—turn out to disappoint as we grow older.

But as I stood on stone steps and looked down on you, I felt your special magic all over again. You're not perfect, San Francisco. But there's no place like you and there never will be.

Especially not for me.
Sincerely,
Ann Cannon

I'LL HAVE A FLYING CAR PLEASE

First Published June 2014

When I was in grade school our family purchased a light green Volkswagen Beetle, and it was the coolest car on the block by far because it could fly.

Yes. You read that correctly.

We had a flying car at our house.

How did we know it was flying car? Because our dad told us so. He dropped the information casually like it was no big deal—like everyone else on our street had flying cars parked in front of their houses, too.

We have a new car and btw it can fly. So yeah. I guess I'll go mow the lawn now.

WAIT! My brothers and I said. OUR CAR CAN FLY?

Our dad assured us this was true, because our car had a "flubber gear" just like the car in that movie about the absent-minded professor. That's how they made cars in Germany. With flubber gears. He said he'd take us for a spin around the neighborhood if we wanted him to, which we did, of course, because come on! Who's going to pass up a chance to fly over your friends' houses in a light green Volkswagen Beetle so you can roll down your window and go "bet your car can't do this, suckers!"

We rushed out of the house and piled into the VW where our dad told us the rules. The car could fly, of course. That's why he bought it. But it would only fly if we closed our eyes and held on tight. If we opened our eyes—even a little bit—we'd crash land, which (of course) would NOT be awesome.

So we closed our eyes and listened as our dad launched the car into orbit. He raced the engine and made whooshing noises and imitated voices of wonder-struck people on the ground below.

It's a bird! It's a plane! Ohmygosh it's a flying Volkswagen!

The ride eventually came to an end. We touched down, opened our eyes and spent the rest of the day telling everybody who would listen about our brand new car. You know. The one that could fly us to the moon.

Years later I would relate this story with mock outrage.

Everybody always says what a great guy my dad is, but seriously! What kind of man would do that to a bunch of innocent little kids? And then I would do a riff or two on how dumb my brothers and I were.

How dumb were we? We were so dumb if you'd asked us which president was buried in Grant's tomb, we would have said Abraham Lincoln. We were so dumb if you'd asked us when the War of 1812 took place, we would have said we didn't know. We were so dumb if you'd asked us if those jokes I just made were funny, we would have laughed some more. And we were so dumb if you'd ask us if cars from Germany could fly, WE WOULD HAVE SAID JAWOHL!

(But only if our eyes were closed.)

The story always got a few laughs, and it still makes me smile. So does my dad. Even in his 80s, that guy still has a knack for bringing the party with him.

Here's another thing. Occasionally when I'm in the mood, I like to look up and imagine what an actual car full of actual kids streaking across the sky might look like.

Ohmygosh, I would say. A flying Volkswagen!

Thanks for that, Dad. You know.

The magic part.

STORY PROBLEMS

First Published June 2013

    I used to hate story problems when I was in grade school. You know. Math problems that involve both numbers AND words—as if somehow math problems with just numbers alone aren't challenging enough.

    I had a hard time with story problems, because I always focused on the wrong elements. Take the following question, for example (which, btw, is an actual problem I just found on a website for school teachers): "You have five mini-pizzas to share with four friends. You're cutting the pizzas in half. How much will each friend get? How can you make sure the leftovers get shared equally?"

    Now if I were still in grade school, I would read this and go, "What kind of toppings do the mini-pizzas have?" or "Hey. Where did they get those mini-pizzas so I can tell my mom to buy some?" or "Wait. If I count myself, there are five kids, so why can't we just all have our own damn mini-pizzas?" or "Who said I had to share the mini-pizzas with my friends anyway? I don't see my friends sharing their mini-pizzas with me!"

See what I mean?

Anyway, I remember the night I asked my dad if he could help me with some homework. He said, sure! Why not? So he took my book and read through the story problems for himself, after which he handed me back my book and said, "I think kids should do their own math, don't you?"

He didn't say so, but I knew my dad didn't see the point of story problems anymore than I did. I also knew that neither he nor my mother was going to do my homework for me. EVER. Homework was my job. And eventually I grew up to be a parent who believed kids should do their own homework, too. As my friend Erynn says, sometimes it's the things we DON'T do for our kids that turn out to be the best gifts we give them.

Still. There are plenty of things my dad did for me over the years. Before I turned 6, he taught how to swim, ride a bike, make a baby laugh, take a wrapper off a popsicle, put salt on an apple, and return a stolen candy bar to the grocery store.

When I was in grade school he taught me how to turn a cartwheel, do a back somersault off the diving board, pick fruit, tell a joke, play Black Magic on road trips and eat tomatoes straight out of the garden.

When I was in high school he taught me how to drive a stick shift, appreciate well-written dialogue in a movie or a television show, and have difficult conversations without resorting to the use of verbal Napalm.

When I became an adult he taught me how to enjoy Hank Williams and Johnny Cash, love a spouse, make a backup plan, deal a deck of cards, call an audible off the field, and accept the fact that there's more than one way to get to the same place.

Or at least he tried to do those things. The truth is I am and I always have been a stubborn student.

Here's another true thing: I didn't do anything to deserve a good dad—anymore than a kid with a bad dad deserves that. I just lucked out in the Dad Department. That's all. Life, unfortunately, is pretty random that way.

But I am grateful for him. Always.

RUNNING SHOES

First Published January 2012

    This is the true story of a pair of shoes and how they changed my life.

    I know! Just like Cinderella! (Only I didn't have to marry a prince and spend the rest of my life going to boring state dinners. Score!)

    It was the spring of 1981. I'd just had our first baby, and I was seriously out of shape.

    How out of shape was I? People, I was so out of shape that I had to hail a cab just to borrow a cup of sugar from our neighbor, Joy, who lived in the apartment across the hallway. Not only that, but the mere act of hailing that cab left me panting with exhaustion. I'd collapse in a nearby chair and moan, "Hailing cabs is such hard work!"

    Then one day, my dad showed up at our door with a pair of running shoes.

    "Here," he said, handing them off to me, "try these on."

    They were Nikes. Air Pegasus, to be exact. And I'd never seen anything like them before, what with their thick-cushioned souls and sleek fabric uppers.

Okay. I'd grown up wearing sneakers—Keds if I was feeling fancy and knockoffs from JCPenney for everything else, including Miss Ercanbrack's seventh-grade gym class where we did squat thrusts (true!) every morning to The Turtles singing, "So Happy Together." But the instant I slipped on the Nikes, I knew I'd soon be thanking my sneakers for the memories and then asking them to move on. For good.

Honey, I felt like I was walking on clouds in those brand new running shoes. I wanted to strap on a big old hoop skirt, stand in front of Tara like Scarlett O'Hara and shout, "As God is my witness, I'll never have shin splints again!" I was so in love with my new running shoes that one day I decided on a whim to—you know—actually run in them. I went outside and jogged about 10 feet before dying of sweatiness. "Wow," I said afterwards, "I'm never doing that again."

Except I did. The very next day. And I increased my distance by another foot. Morning after morning after morning I did this, until one day I discovered that I had signed up for a local road race, in which I ran and in which I did not finish dead last.

That was 30 years ago, and I've been (kinda) running more or less regularly ever since. I don't run fast, and I don't run pretty. In fact, I suspect I look like that person you see struggling on the side of the road sometimes when you're driving around town—the person who makes you want to roll down your window and shout, "Dude! Give it up! You're just embarrassing yourself and also the rest of mankind!" Still. I keep at it. On good days, running makes me feel like I'm 10 years old again, tearing barefoot around our backyard and playing night games with the neighbor kids on a warm

July evening. That's not a bad feeling when you're 56 and there's a lot of January going on outside your window.

The reason I bring this all up is that by the time you read today's paper, I'll be in southern California, preparing to run Disneyland's Tinkerbell Half-Marathon. I assume I'll get passed up by a lot of wacky fun-loving gals wearing wings and tutus while I toil (not in wings and tutu) to post the slowest land speed records known to man.

It'll be fun, though. Possibly. Or not. But whatever, because it's too late now.

Meanwhile, as I run beneath a canopy of palms, I'll think about how one gift from an unlikely fairy godmother, a.k.a "my dad," can sometimes take a person down miles (and miles!) of unexpected roads.

MEMORIAL DAY

First Published May 2012

    I remember the time I was at an event with my family when the emcee asked all audience members who'd served in the armed forces to stand up. My dad took to his feet, and I had one of those moments when I went, "Oh yeah, that's right. He was in the army."

    My dad is many things to me: a parent, a gardener, a reader of thrillers, a music lover, a Willy Nelson fanboy, an avid golfer, an expert in the fine art of dealing cards, an agreeable conversationalist over an order of chips and salsa, a surprising friend to poodles. But I never think of him as a soldier. Which he was. And so this year for Memorial Day, I decided to ask him a few questions about his experiences, lest I forget. Again.

ME: You signed up for ROTC when you were at a student at Utah State. Why?

DAD: It was compulsory at USU, which was a land-grant college. Every male student had to take two years of ROTC. Meanwhile, the Korean War broke out, so I signed up for two more years—Advanced ROTC—partly because they paid you. Twenty-five dollars was a lot of money to me back then. When you graduated you owed the government two years of service.

ME: What rank were you when you graduated and entered the service?

DAD: The day I graduated from college I had my commission—I was a second lieutenant in the United States Army with orders to report to Fort Lee, Virginia. A friend I'd played football with in college, Jimmy Garrett, [who later became a scout for the Dallas Cowboys and whose son Jason is currently the Cowboys' head coach] got me on the team as soon as I arrived. A lot of bases had football teams at that time because so many soldiers had been playing college ball when the conflict broke out.

While I was at Fort Lee, I had to take a six-week course where we went bivouacking in the woods. They were trying to turn guys like me into actual officers. I also took a course in food services.

ME: Seriously? Food services? The only thing I ever remember you making at home when we were growing up was oatmeal.

DAD: I know, right? And then I was sent to Fort Mead where it was my job to arrange courses in food services to the enlisted men who all knew at least 100 times more than I did.

ME: I really, really cannot picture any of this.

DAD: I was the head football coach of the Fort Mead team. We won our first three games but lost our fourth. The next thing I knew I had my overseas orders. I lost one game, and I was out of there. Talk about a tough alumnae.

ME: You went to Japan, right?

DAD: Yeah. I was surprised by the orders, because by then actual hostilities had ceased. But there were still troops there.

It was a rough boat ride to Japan. It took 16 days, and I was sick for 14 of them. When I got there, I worked at the R and R center.

ME: Oh. That's where Hawkeye and Trapper John went on their vacations, right?

DAD: (ignoring me) We'd feed the men on leave a big steak dinner as soon as they got there, even if it was at midnight. We'd feed them all week. And then when they left after seven days, we'd feed them another steak dinner.

ME: What was it like to be in Japan with your bride back home, working in a bank?

DAD: My time abroad was uneventful. But being away was hard. There you are—off in a whole new country and culture by yourself. You're lonely. I just have so much respect for all these young men and women today who ship out for places like Afghanistan. Think of your boys, Ann, facing the dangers those kids face every day.

I do think of it—especially on Memorial Day, which was created to remember those who have served in any and all capacities. Thank you.

And if the opportunity presents itself this weekend to ask your own soldiers to share their memories, do it.

MENTAL ILLNESS

First Published April 2015

    The news that a German co-pilot deliberately crashed an airbus full of passengers into a mountainside is horrifying. It's been difficult to read about it, to imagine the last terrible moments when many of those passengers realized they were taking their last breaths. And now the rest of us are left behind to ask why—just as we always do in the face of another unspeakable tragedy.

    Much of the discussion in the aftermath of the catastrophe has focused on the mental state of the young man responsible for the murder of so many innocent people. And what we've discovered is that the co-pilot had a mental illness rap sheet.

    I always receive this kind of information with a sinking heart because of the reaction people inevitably have. Mentally ill individuals are not to be trusted because they fly airplanes into mountains! Or shoot up movie theaters! Or take students hostage! And without even realizing it, we have one more reason to distance ourselves from people who suffer from mental illnesses. We have one more reason to see them as the "other"—individuals who are different, who stand apart and mean us harm.

When I was growing up, stories about crazed escapees from the local mental hospital were slumber party staples, just like stories about Ouija boards or graveyard Weeping Marys. I once told my father one of these stories when I was in junior high school and I'll never forget his reaction. He just shook his head and said, "Honey, most people with mental illness are no different than you and me."

I didn't fully understand or appreciate what he was saying then. But I do now.

Here's the thing. Like many of you, I have seen firsthand what mental illness can do to an individual and to the people who love that individual. Please believe me when I say I have more than a casual acquaintance with the suffering mental illness causes—especially if the illness goes undiagnosed or untreated. The pain and collateral damage can be harrowing. A close friend of ours who has suffered a great deal of physical hurt in his life maintains that his periodic bouts of clinical depression are far worse than broken bones. It's hard to move when despair is whistling through your head.

And yet so many people who do suffer from mental illnesses keep fighting to get out of bed, go to work, pay their bills, take care of their families, love their friends, read a book, check their email, watch a ball game, wash a car, prepare and eat a meal, search for something that will make them laugh, stand quiet on the front porch to marvel at the returning sound of birdsong in a spring tree.

That's what they do. They just keep fighting. And for every mentally ill person who does the unthinkable, there are so, so many more who will never be a headline, who will never be a news story.

I honor their grit and the courage of the people who love them.

GREEN LIGHTS

First Published April 2014

    Good morning, *Tribune* readers! Peabody here. I'd like you to step into the WABAC machine with my boy, Sherman, and me so that you can see how automobiles used to respond at intersections with stoplights.

    Ready? Excellent!

    Yes. Here we are! The year is 1972. Richard Nixon is in the White House calling the shots. Marlon Brando is on the big screen with cotton in his mouth, making people offers they can't refuse. Steve McGarrett is on TV, keeping the streets of Honolulu safe. Jane Fonda is in Hanoi, bonding with the North Vietnamese. Michael Jackson is on the radio singing a song about someone named Ben, who's a rat. Literally.

    Meanwhile, Ann Cannon is in Utah County, learning how to drive a car and also making her father wish that teenage girls had never been invented!

    In particular, Ann's father objects to the way she responds whenever they approach an intersection. Just the other day she kept right on going, even though her father told her TO STOP because the light was yellow. Ann is like that sometimes—disinclined to listen to hysterical fathers in passenger seats. But on this occasion (Ann and her father were headed to Carson's Market to collect the deposit on empty pop bottles) she could tell he really, really, really meant it.

So she slammed on the brakes. In the middle of the intersection. Thus pitching her father (and approximately 1000 empty bottles) into the windshield. For as long as she lives, Ann will never forget what her father looked like with approximately 1000 empty bottles sailing past his ears. "WHY DID YOU STOP IN THE MIDDLE OF THE INTERSECTION?" He asked her. Pointedly. Also loudly. "Because you told me, too," she said. "Duh."

Dads! What's their deal anyway?

But whatever.

The problem is that Ann hates to sit still, which is why she doesn't usually stop for yellow lights. It's also the reason she likes to gun the engine and race like a jackrabbit on Adderall out into the intersection as soon as the light turns green.

She's not the only driver who does this. In 1972, everyone puts the pedal to the metal as soon as the light changes. It's like the beginning of the Indy 500, right there at the intersection of Center Street and University Avenue.

Remember those days? When cars actually moved as soon as the light changed?

Now you have to wait at an intersection after a light changes. You have to wait, wait, and also wait. Sometimes you even have to honk your horn to tell the driver in front of you to get a move on after the light turns green. Sometimes you even have to honk your horn at the same driver over and over as the two of you hit every intersection along Ninth East.

So what's changed?

Thanks to my massive, super-smart Peabody dog brain I have discovered the answer, which is this: back in 1972, drivers weren't pulling out their cell phones to check for messages every time they stopped at a traffic light. Cell phones hadn't been invented yet. So drivers just sat in their cars and listened to Michael Jackson sing love songs to his pet rat.

Ben, the two of us need look no more.

We both found what we were looking for . . .

AAUGH! No wonder drivers were in a hurry to get moving again. But that's not the point. The point is this: absolutely NOBODY needs to check for email or text messages while driving a car. Please let them wait. So I don't have to.

Sincerely,
Mr. Peabody

HANK WILLIAMS

I love this story about Dad.

When he used to recruit as a young assistant in the Bay Area—Walnut Creek, San Leandro, Hayward, Fremont—he would drive into San Francisco at night and go to places like the Hungry Eye and Tommy's Joint. Real '60s places where the music flowed through the venue like light flows through a window. It didn't matter to him that he was alone. He just wanted to hear music. Live.

I was reminded of this when we went through my parents' storage unit. There was a treasure trove of vinyl and WOW! The variety! Jazz. Pop. Folk. Show tunes, including the sound track from *West Side Story*.

Oh, *West Side Story*.

Dad used to roll his eyes if anybody brought up my youthful obsession with WSS. The year I was sick, my parents moved the phonograph into my bedroom and let me choose what I wanted to listen to.

Which was WSS. Period. Except when it was Christmas. Then I wanted to listen to Alvin and the Chipmunks.

I was only 6 years old—a sick little white girl with kidney disease from Utah—but somehow that soundtrack just spoke to me. I was there on the playground with my boys, singing and snapping my fingers and itching for the next rumble.

Neither of my parents complained THEN about the way I played WSS over and over and over again. And also over again. They just let the lyrics roll down the hallway from my bedroom throughout the house like the tumbleweeds that rolled down the street in front of our house.

It was only later that I learned that not everyone wanted to be a Jet when they grew up.

Or a Shark.

So back to Dad and music. I don't think he ever wanted to create music himself on the instruments he admires, i.e. the guitar and the banjo. He was in the mixed choir in his high school but (true story) the choir director told Dad he'd get an A if he just mouthed the words at the Christmas concert.

No. He was like the voracious reader who has no desire to write a novel himself.

For him music is there to enjoy. Enjoyment is his talent—one he passed along to my brothers and me.

EXCEPT. When I was in high school, I hate hate hated country western music. To openly admit that you liked CW when I was in high school would have been the equivalent of committing social Hari-kari. It was the early '70s and hard rock ruled the airwaves of Provo, Utah. Led Zeppelin. Uriah Heep. Led Zeppelin. Black Sabbath. Led Zeppelin. Deep Purple. Led Zeppelin.

Also Led Zeppelin.

We saw ourselves as being urban. Ironic. Cynical. Certainly much more sophisticated than our peers to the immediate south in Springville and Spanish Fork and to the north in Pleasant Grove and American Fork. Those towns were still rural, homes to 4H clubs and FFA, said us Provo High snobs. Those kids from Spanish Fork could have their CW. We were dopers. Not ropers.

Or whatever.

So I was having absolutely ZERO of it when Dad dropped his Hank Williams LPs on the turntable.

Ugh, I said.

What, he said.

This music. It's awful, I said.

Awful? I'll tell you what. It's the music of the people.

Which people? Not my people.

You're my people. I'm your people. This is your music, too.

Ugh, I said.

And so the two of us would have at it. Back and forth and back and forth and back and forth.

And then one afternoon, many years later, I caught the sound of Hank singing about train whistles and I'll tell you what. The pureness of that melancholy voice straight up stopped the breath in my throat.

You're right, Dad, I said to the air.

I get it now.

FATHERS AND FATHERS

First Published June 2015

What with Father's Day right around the corner, I've been thinking a lot about moms.

Kidding!

I've been thinking about dads, obv—especially the dads I have known. My own father, my husband, my grandfathers, my brothers, my sons, my friends' dads. Memories roll in like waves, tossing up fragments of themselves like bits of shell and sea glass for me to examine.

This morning I awoke thinking of the time my dad and I picked up his father from the care facility where he spent the last few months of his life to take him for a ride on a bright Sunday afternoon. We drove around the streets of Provo and Orem, which had changed so much since he'd arrived in Utah Valley from Buckhorn Flat as a young man with a sixth-grade education who hoped to grow trees and to "peddle" (his word) fruit.

I like to think of what Utah Valley looked like in the days of my grandfather's youth, dotted with green groves of cherry, apple, and pear trees. And peach trees, too—my favorites with their frilly dress blossoms and their long elegant leaves.

It's hard to say, though, if my grandfather even remembered his own orchards that afternoon as we drove together through the terraced foothills. He sat in the passenger seat looking with delighted surprise out the window, as though he'd never seen his own town before. I remember thinking how sweet-natured, how cheerful he was in that moment, as though all the best parts of him had been distilled into some deep, defining good will toward everything he saw.

Toward the end of our car ride, I noticed my grandfather looking closely at my father. A slow smile spread across his face and he shook his finger as though he'd just understood the punch line of a joke he'd heard a few minutes earlier.

"I know who you are," he said finally. "You're the one who played basketball."

Here's the thing. My grandfather had seven athletic sons who all played ball in high school. And while it's true that my dad played some basketball at Lincoln High School, what he really played was football. In fact, he ended up with a scholarship to play football at Utah State where he went on to graduate—the first in his family to attend college. And after that he earned a masters degree. And after that he earned an Ed.D. All because he played football.

But there in the car my dad fully matched his own father's proud smile and said, "Yup. You're right. I'm the one who played basketball."

I witnessed something special that day, although I was too young to fully appreciate it at the time. What I saw was a father playing father to his son. And a son playing father to his father.

Life goes on and along the way things change. Orchards

give way to neighborhoods and old family roles—father, son, mother, daughter, brother and sister—give way to new ones. And for me, at least, those changes are often hard.

But when I think of my father and grandfather on that sunny drive so long ago, I know that while things change—that indeed they must change—it is possible for kindness to endure.

HOW TO BE PRESENT WHEN SOMEONE'S WORLD FALLS APART

So okay. Maybe that title is a little heavy on the melodrama.

But still.

That's how I felt when I experienced my first major depressive episode in my early 20s.

I was teaching high school and it wasn't going well. I'm not sure that rocky first year triggered the emotional avalanche that buried me, but it sure didn't help. I couldn't eat. I couldn't sleep. And eventually I couldn't feel. I spent a fair amount of time wishing I were dead, frankly.

Nobody recognized this version of Ann. I didn't recognize her myself. It's not that I was always happy before. It wasn't like I was Maria Von Trapp, singing songs and making children's clothing out of curtains. For one thing, I can't sing. For another, I can't sew. But at least I'd been a person who was engaged with the world.

Until I wasn't.

It was my principal, a grand man named John Matthews, who realized something was seriously wrong with me. He'd seen what clinical depression looked like up close and personal in his own family. So John called my father.

In retrospect, I find it interesting that he called Dad instead of my young husband of less than two years. My guess is that he was acting out of a good father's instinct to protect a daughter and that at some level he understood my parents were in a better position than a young frightened spouse to deal with the challenge of a wife who was ill.

So here's what my parents did, God bless them. They found a psychiatrist and made an appointment. And for the next six months, I saw that doctor regularly. Our visits weren't long. Mostly the doctor explained what was happening and reassured me that I would get better if I just took my meds and hung in there. He also made me feel less alone, less freakish, which was a huge blessing in the 1970s before everybody went public with their mental health issues.

Just knowing that other people had also felt like nothing more than skin stretched over the hollow inside gave me comfort.

Here's something else that helped.

In the early weeks of my treatment, my parents drove me to the doctor's office. They were worried that I couldn't or wouldn't make it there on my own. Because my appointments were in the early afternoon, this meant Dad often left the practice field and drove me there.

I remember walking out of the doctor's office and seeing him standing in the half-light of the hallway.

Waiting for me.

WHAT I MISS

After Dad retired people asked what I missed the most about Football World Up Close and Personal.

The games?

No. Not really. They were loads of fun when we were winning. But they could also be torture when we weren't. "It's only a game" isn't quite true for a coach and a coach's family. There's a lot riding on games. Like job security.

So, no. I don't miss the games. I still watch some college football and a LOT of pro ball, and because I don't have so much invested in a game's outcome, I can sit back and enjoy. You know. Like a regular fan.

What I do miss, though, is what happened after a game.

After a game we'd gather outside the locker room door to wait for Dad to emerge. Typically he was one of the last to emerge, following a string of freshly showered players, equipment managers, assistant coaches, grad assistants, sportswriters and team doctors.

Finally he'd appear like a rumpled bear from a cave at the first hint of spring. He always wore a hat—a golf hat if the weather was warm, a stocking cap if it wasn't. And he always had a sack lunch tucked under his arm, which he shared with the kids—at least the chips and the candy bars. He'd save the sandwich for himself, unwrapping it as stadium security opened the gate to let us onto the field.

He'd start eating the sandwich and talking a little about the game as we all made our way across the field to the press box where he'd do his call-in show while still eating a sandwich.

It's funny the things you miss after they're gone. Our walks across the field were so habitual, so routine, that I took them for granted. They were as much a part of our lives as breathing.

But now I find myself wishing I could stand on that empty field again after a game so that its scent, thick and pungent and warm, could rise up around my legs in the cool of an autumn evening's mist.

DEVAN

First Published September 2014

    I've told you this story before, right?
    The one about my brothers and me and what horrible teeth we all had when we were little? Our teeth were so bad our parents would have had to refinance the house just to pay for dental work.
    Here's what my parents did instead. Whenever our dad had business in northern California, he'd pile us kids into the station wagon and take us with him. Along the way we'd stop at his old college buddy's dentist office in San Leandro where DeVan "Doc" Robins took care of our teeth for free—usually on a Sunday afternoon when the office was otherwise empty.
    DeVan was a one-man show on the days we straggled into his office. He was the receptionist, hygienist, assistant, lab tech, and dentist all rolled up into one large, jolly bundle. In fact, I had no idea that people like "hygienists" and "dental assistants" really existed until I grew up and went to dentists in Utah. I thought they were mythical creatures. Like hobbits, for example.

Here was the other amazing thing about DeVan. He could work on your teeth anywhere. DeVan often worked on my dad's mouth (he had bad teeth, too) in the parking lot after a football game. Once he checked Dad's teeth in front of a restaurant before they went inside to eat. They had a deal, DeVan and Dad. My father was supposed to save DeVan's soul and DeVan was supposed to save my father's teeth.

DeVan always said he was the one with the harder job.

Here's the thing I didn't know about DeVan until I attended his funeral on Saturday. You know all that work he did for us when my parents were young and still struggling financially? He did the same thing for plenty of other people, too, over the course of his long career. And when he retired, he set up a chair in his home, partly so he could keep seeing those former patients who couldn't afford dental care. He and his amazing wife, Ruby, were generous to the core.

My father spoke at DeVan's funeral and as I listened to him tell stories—tender and funny—I remembered something my grandfather once said to me. It's a hard, hard thing to outlive a friend, he told me, especially a friend who's a peer—someone who listened to the same music as you did, who rode in the same car and lived through the same wars and watched the same movies and wore his hair the same way and knew the same girls and played in the same games on a September afternoon when the air was crisp and the hills to the east blazed with color and the two of you had your whole lives stretching ahead of you like an endless ribbon of road.

It's hard to lose someone like that.

But at the same time weren't DeVan and my dad so lucky to have found one another when they were young and then to have remained friends for the wave of years that followed? In the words of the poet Hilaire Belloc, both of them could say " for no one . . . had quite such pleasant friends as mine, or

loved them half as much as I did."
    Love your friends, people.
    Love your friends.

SAFE PASSAGE

First Published December 2016

True Story.

When I was an English major at BYU my dad told me to tell my professors that I was his daughter. I was appalled.

"Seriously, Dad?" I said. "You think I'm gonna start dropping your name now?"

His name was LaVell Edwards and it was a point of honor with me not to play the LaVell card.

He looked at me with this expression he used to get on his face—crooked smile, one eye half-closed, his look all wry and sly.

"Hey," he said. "I've got a bunch of players who need all the help they can get in the English department over there. I need YOU to help ME."

Now here's another true story.

I was sitting in a room once, the only woman in a room full of men, when I realized that no one there was really listening to what I was saying. The guys were talking over me, around me, past me. And suddenly I realized I was having an experience I had never had before, i.e. not being listened to because I was—you know—a girl.

Here's the thing. My dad always listened to me. He listened to me as much as he listened to my brothers. Daughter. Sons. Sons. Daughter. It was all the same to him. In a world that sometimes values its boys more than its girls, that man gave me the gift of taking me seriously.

And also not seriously.

My dad loved to laugh. And he loved anyone who made him laugh. Laughing LaVell was a thing of beauty. Here's what he looked like. First, he would close his eyes and crinkle up his face. Then he would throw back his head and clap his hands. And THEN came the noise—an explosion of mirth that made his shoulders shake.

I loved that sound, and so when I was a little girl I would make jokes to see if I could get him to laugh. Stupid jokes. Lame jokes. But I would always wait for the reaction, and when it came—which it usually did because he was a generous laugher—I felt buoyant.

Here's a little heads-up for all you dads out there. Do your daughters a favor and laugh at their jokes. Go to their parent teacher conferences. Treat their mothers and grandmothers with respect. Teach them how to do the things that you know how to do—swing a golf club, throw a softball, make a garden, love Willie Nelson with all your heart and soul, drive a stick shift, tell a story while sitting on the living room couch, help a stranger, salt an apple, swim the length of a pool, be there for a friend, try something new, write little notes of encouragement, always deal face cards to your left, withhold judgment, sing along with the radio even if you can't sing, feed your wife's dog the rest of your dinner when your wife isn't looking, cry at your daughter's wedding, and smile whenever you step away from the sidelines.

The lessons you teach her may not always take.
But she won't forget that you tried.
Safe passage, Dad.

FUNERAL TALK

Before I begin, I'd like to acknowledge all the loving kindness we've received over the past few weeks.

Thanks to our large extended family—all the aunts, uncles, cousins, and in-laws who were a sweet part of my father's big, rich life.

Thanks to Bishop Brian Santiago and the rest of the Oak Hills 6th ward, including the Relief Society sisters who've prepared a meal for our family today and the deacons who visited on Sundays to share the sacrament with my parents.

Thanks to his former players and coaches and co-workers, including Shirley Johnson.

Thanks to Drs. Kendell Cannon, Gary Garner, Cameron Kessler and Marv Allen for their end-of-life care. Thanks, as well, to caregivers Tammy, Adrienne, and Mahana.

Thanks to Sundberg-Olpin Mortuary for their good work.

And a heartfelt thanks to each and every one of you today who have traveled near and far to be with us. Our gratitude truly knows no limits.

In the fall of 1950 LaVell Edwards, a member of the Utah State University football team, was asked to help select new members for the school's Sponsor Corps—a paramilitary organization whom the *Herald Journal* described as consisting of fierce females "dressed in snappy powder-blue uniform and berets." The *Herald Journal* went on to note that when performing at the annual Cherry Blossom Festival in the late 1950s these coeds "wheeled, turned and presented arms with such spit-and-polish that they won 10th place in a field of more than 30 college drill teams."

So okay. The Sponsor Corps was not really a paramilitary organization. It was, as noted, a drill team, which is why LaVell the Football Player was invited to cast a vote. And when a certain new co-ed, a former rodeo queen from Big Piney, Wyoming took center stage to twirl a rifle, LaVell sat up and took note.

Who was this vision of precision, he wondered? He had to find out. And he soon learned that her name was Patti Louise Covey—the only child of Irwin and Louise Covey who ran a garage and gas station on the corner of Highway 189 and the only grandchild of a truly terrifying woman named PattI (AUTHOR'S NOTE: Yes, she capped the "i") Larsen who slept with a shotgun when she wasn't busy acting as Sublette County's game warden.

Actually Patti's father, who wasn't a member of the Mormon church at the time, expressed his reluctance when Patti left to attend college. Like any good citizen of Wyoming, he had little fondness for the citizens of Utah. When she left he said plaintively, "Sis, I hate to send you down to Utah where you'll probably marry one of those damn Mormon boys—a LaVar, LaMar, LaDell, LaVell or a Garth."

LaVell began to pursue Patti with the same tenacity that

had characterized his play as an All-State linebacker when he was student at Orem's old Lincoln High School.

But sly Patti initially dodged his pursuit with a few sweet moves of her own. She canceled a date with him so she go to the Rainbow Rendezvous in Salt Lake City with someone else. She introduced him at a gathering as LaDell Anderson instead of LaVell Edwards. In general, she played hard to get LIKE A BOSS. Which, of course, only served to further pique LaVell's interest.

Along the way, however, she secretly started to notice LaVell. Even though she didn't care for the way he trudged around campus in galoshes during the winter months—she thought they made him look silly and seriously who can blame a girl for thinking that—Patti began to do her LaVell homework.

She knew absolutely nothing about football and, in fact, had no desire to actually attend a game herself. But her roommate was a football fanatic. This roommate went to every single home game and then reported back to Patti, describing in vivid detail everything LaVell, who played center on offense, had done. So by the time LaVell and Patti actually began dating, he was totally blown away by her "knowledge," because (as he was fond of saying) absolutely no one but a center's mother pays attention to what a center does during a game.

It wasn't until after they were married that Patti confessed to LaVell that she had never seen him play. Ah. True confessions are rarely—if ever—a good idea.

But don't worry. LaVell made the unfortunate mistake of coming clean himself. On their honeymoon, Patti asked LaVell who he thought was prettier—Patti or another sorority girl they both knew. LaVell gave the question some earnest thought. And then he naively responded, "Well, she has a better face, but you have a better body."

In spite of early moments like these, Patti and LaVell forged a wonderful partnership that lasted for 65 years. He loved her for her intelligence, her loyalty, her great sense of fun, her talent for making and sustaining friendships and her deep desire to do the right thing. During their time together, they both weathered and embraced a mix of everything Life has to offer—including a lengthy separation during the Korean War, the much wanted births of three children, the protracted illness of a young daughter, demanding church callings, grueling work schedules that involved a good deal of time away from home, loooooong road trips with three kids, a succession of pets including a pair of hamsters that disappeared in the house and were never seen or heard from again, a glorious run of championships, some disappointing losses, the deaths of parents and siblings, good times with great friends on the golf course and around a card table, a couples mission to New York City and annual beach trips with children, grandchildren, and great-grandchildren.

Patti was a huge part of LaVell's singular success as a coach. And he knew it. He often told me that it was such a relief to him that he never had to worry about what was happening at home when he was gone because Patti had things firmly in hand.

The assistant coaches and players, as well as their girlfriends and wives, know that Patti was instrumental in LaVell's success, too. She has a genius for sensing what people need and reaching out to them. On a national level, she was the driving force behind the American Football Coaches Wives Association, an organization that offers support to the families whose lives are defined by a sometimes brutal profession, as well as doing good works in communities around the nation.

On the local level, she is the driving force behind an annual golf tournament designed to raise money for the charity of her choice—The Boys and Girls Clubs of Utah County. Her community activism makes her family proud.

Thank you for giving me an opportunity to make this tribute to tough and tender Patti Louise Covey Edwards. I know our father approves, because, Mom, he loves you so.

How could he not?

In conclusion, because our father always wished he were at least a tiny bit Irish, I think it's appropriate to share with you all an Irish blessing.

May the road rise up to meet you,
May the wind always be at your back,
May the sun shine warm upon your face,
The rain fall soft upon your fields,
And until we meet again,
May God hold you in the hollow of his hand.

PEACHES

First Published October 2017

    It's October now, so I think we've pretty much seen the last of the local peaches for sale at the corner fruit stands, right? Except, of course, for a few peach outliers.
    Anyway, for six-eight weeks as late summer morphs into early autumn here along the Wasatch Front, I eat fresh peaches like. It's. My. Job. I don't discriminate. I am an equal opportunity peach employer. If you are a peach, I will find a place for you in my life. Suncrest. O'Henry. Red Haven. Angelus. Elberta. Do you hear that, peaches? I love you all.
    Did I get my fill of peaches this season? Of course not. I never do. But at least I was on my game, unlike last year.
    What can I say about this time last year? That it was hard? Yes. That is was tender? Of course. That our family knew we were headed for that moment when our lives would be reordered? Yes. That, too. It was clear to all of us who loved him that my father's health was failing fast.
    He'd had a bad summer, so I started driving down to Provo regularly to be with him and my mother. We'd spend

time in the family room where Dad would sit in his chair close to the fireplace because, even though it was August, he was often cold. We'd talk about the people he knew and he'd tell stories. Some of them I'd heard before, like the ones about his old Lincoln High School football coach, Sanky Dixon. Some of them were new to me, like the one about the time he and his friends stole into a neighbor's chicken coop, only to be discovered by the good-natured neighbor himself who didn't seem to be the least a) surprised or b) angered by the sight of kids in the chicken coop at midnight.

Meanwhile, whenever Mom would leave she'd say, "Don't let your father give the rest of his lunch to the dog." And then as soon as she'd walk out the door, he'd give the rest of his lunch to the dog.

"Don't tell your mother," he'd say. The problem is that food just didn't taste good to him anymore, he'd say.

Except for the peaches.

Bottled peaches tasted especially good to him, which was a change. The son of a truck farmer, he'd always preferred fruit fresh. But then everything was changing. So Mom broke out her old-timey canning skills and lined their kitchen counter with jars full of sliced amber fruit floating in sweet rosy liquid.

One day when we were watching an old movie—I watched a lot of old movies last summer, which led me to conclude that not every film made during Hollywood's golden era was actually golden—I told Dad I was disappointed in myself.

Why, he asked.

Because I didn't eat enough peaches this year, I told him. And now the season is almost over. Sad face!

Later that day, Dad slipped out of the house. When he returned he held a small white paper bag—the kind with a handle—full of the season's last peaches. Peach outliers.

Here, he said. These are for you.

People, of course, are often remembered for the big things they did in this life.

But, in the end, it's the small gestures that define who they really were.

YOUR PEOPLE STAY WITH YOU

First Published June 2017

 So the thing of it is this: if you live long enough, you're going to lose people you love. It's as inevitable as a freak snowstorm during spring vacation in Utah. Like Johnny Cash said, the man comes around. For all of us.
 But what I've come to realize is that the people I've lost are still with me because of the things I do and say as a result of having known them when they were alive.
 Take my friend Marilyn, for example. Marilyn was one of those big personalities with a big heart (cliché, I know, but accurate) and big opinions about everything. She loved Barbra Streisand, romantic comedies, pieced quilts, poodles, Nalley's chili from a can, limited-edition dipped Oreos, silver rings on every finger, and her collectible teddy bears. She began most of her sentences in a husky smoker's voice with the phrase, "the thing of it is," which is a great way to start a column, too. Thanks for that, Marilyn.

Speaking of great phrases, my great-grandmother had a few of her own. I do have personal memories of her—I keep a picture of us eating Christmas dinner together by my bedside--but by then she was a frail tamer version of her essential self. In her prime she'd been the game warden of Sublette County, Wyoming, a force of nature big enough to intimidate my father whom she attempted to teach how to fish. It didn't work. My dad stood on the banks of a glittering river, accidentally casting off in the shrubs behind him and getting his line tangled up everywhere. Domestic chaos was her preferred environment but occasionally she attempted to impose order. "I'm going to get lined up today," she'd say. And although she's been gone for years, both my mother and I say the same thing. "I'm going to get lined up today." Thanks for that, Grandma Pat.

When I was growing up I was nuts about horses but didn't have the opportunity to ride much so I read books by Marguerite Henry instead. When I married my husband, his father, who was nuts enough about horses to actually own them, took me for rides in the foothills above Provo. He also taught me how to drive a pony cart. So if you need someone to drive a pony cart to the grocery store for you, I'm your girl. Thanks for that, Kenneth.

And then there was my friend Becky. We discovered each other at church when we were 10 years old. I still remember the first time I saw her, standing there in the hallway with her yellow hair and her yellow dress, saying hello to me first because I was shy and she wasn't. We talked every day for years. She reminded me of C.S. Lewis's description of his mother, a woman who took to happiness like some people take to the best seat on a train. That is NOT my natural tendency. But I try to give it a decent shot. Thanks for that, Becky.

Last February descended heavy on me like a curtain of gloom. I didn't want to get out of bed. It was dark. And cold. And if there is anything I hate, hate, hate in this life, it's being cold. But then I remembered something my dad always used to say. "As long as my neck is warm, the rest of me stays warm."

So I crawled out of bed, wrapped a scarf around my neck, and carried on.

Thanks for that, Dad.

Acknowledgments

Wow!

I'm so glad these columns have found a place to live between the covers of this book. Many thanks to Anne Holman for suggesting that The King's English Bookshop take on this project. Speaking of The King's English, I want to thank Betsy Burton for her support and also for hiring me (pretty much on a whim!) all those years ago. The store and its staff are home and family to me.

Speaking some more of The King's English, I want to give Jamie Ortwein and Rob Eckman so much love for the hours they put into making I'll Tell You What... happen. Also, what would I have done without AB Brillinger's brilliant eyes on this? And thanks, too, for Joanie Packard's skills with graphics.

Thank you, as well, to The Salt Lake Tribune for publishing most of these columns in the first place and for agreeing to let us reprint them. I especially want to thank the editors I've worked with—Lisa Carricaburu, Anna Cekola, Jennifer Napier-Pearce, and Terry Orme.

Finally, I want to thank my marvelous family for letting me exploit them week after week as I wrote these columns. Thank you, Phil and Kendell, Alec and Randi, Dylan and Julie, Geoffrey, and Quinton and Cami. Thanks to my brothers, Johnny and Jimmy, and their families. Thanks to the Cannon clan and their families. Thanks especially to my parents, LaVell and Patti Edwards.

And thank you most of all to Ken Cannon. You made me a writer.

Ann Edwards on a pony at Knott's Berry Farm, shortly before her parents lost her. But that's another story.

CPSIA information can be obtained
at www.ICGtesting.com
Printed in the USA
FSHW02n0817090518
47805FS

9 781532 353376